GRAND

Moments

GRAND
Moments
Devotions Inspired
by Grandkids

LYDIA E. HARRIS

AMG
PUBLISHERS

GRAND Moments: Devotions Inspired by Grandkids

ISBN: 978-1-61715-597-0

This author is represented by the literary agency of WordServe Literary, www.wordserveliterary.com.

Editing and typesetting by Rick Steele Editorial Services, Ringgold, GA (https://steeleeditorialservices.myportfolio.com)

Author photos used on back cover and on page ix, courtesy of GlimmerGlass Photography, Seattle, WA

Recipes excerpted from: *In the Kitchen with Grandma.* Copyright © 2019 Lydia E. Harris. Published by Harvest House Publishers, Eugene, Oregon 97408. www.harvesthousepublishers.com

Cover Design by BookBaby (BookBaby.com), Pennsauken, NJ

Printed in the United States of America

Dedication

Dedicated with love to our grandchildren and their
godly parents:

Steve and Anita Faull and their sons,
Peter and Alex,

and

Jon and Amy Harris and their children,
Clara, Owen, and Anna

We thank God for each of you.

Also dedicated with gratitude to our grandchildren's
other grandparents.

Don and Cheryl Faull
and
Gordon and Judy Kelly

God bless you all.

Acknowledgments

This devotional book is a gift of love to you from many people.

I would like to thank my family, friends, and fellow writers, who offered encouragement, prayers, quotes to include, and helped me throughout the writing process.

Also, thanks to my husband, Milt, for his prayers and loving support as president of my Fan Club.

I couldn't have completed this book without your help.

Special thanks to:

Nick Harrison and Greg Johnson of WordServe Literary Agency

Mary A. Hake and Rick Steele for editing

Amanda Jenkins and AMG Publishers

Most of all, to God be the glory!

About the Author

LYDIA E. HARRIS began writing for publication in her fifties and later published her Bible study, *Preparing My Heart for Grandparenting*, with AMG Publishers. Lydia also enjoys creating and taste-testing recipes with her grandchildren. Her recipes have been published in Focus on the Family's *Clubhouse Jr*, *Clubhouse*, and *Brio* magazines and in her cookbook, *In the Kitchen with Grandma: Stirring Up Tasty Memories Together*, published by Harvest House Publishers. She has also published many stories and devotions in periodicals and compilation books.

Lydia has penned the column "A Cup of Tea with Lydia" for *The Country Register* newspapers in the US and Canada for more than twenty years. (It's no wonder her grandkids call her "Grandma Tea.") Together, Lydia and her husband, Milt, are intentional about passing on a legacy of faith to their two married children and five grandchildren. She is passionate about prayer and grandparenting and is eager to inspire other grandparents to pass the baton of faith to their children and grandchildren.

GRAND Moments: Devotions Inspired by Grandkids

Contents

Contents

Contents

Contents

For further reading: the devotions in each section relate to the topics in *Preparing My Heart for Grandparenting,* a Bible study written by Lydia E. Harris and published by AMG Publishers (2010).

Introduction

God blessed my husband, Milt, and me with five "joybringers"—as we call our grandchildren. Now, it is a joy to share with you *GRAND Moments*, devotions inspired by our grandchildren and God's Word.

A Book Is Born

When our first grandchild, Peter, was born, so was Grandma Tea. (My daughter gave me that name because I write a tea column and love all things tea.) I began recording lessons learned from Peter and the grandchildren that followed—Alex, Clara, Owen, and Anna. After we spent time together, I would ask God if there were insights from them and His Word that He wanted me to learn. When God answered with a yes, I recorded these thoughts and tried to apply the lessons to my life. And so, the idea for this book was born.

Memories to Treasure

Grandkids grow up fast, and today my "joybringers" range in age from thirteen to twenty-four years. In *GRAND Moments*, I share treasured stories coupled with spiritual connections from different ages and stages of my grandchildren's lives. These are arranged by topics rather than in chronological order, and the topics relate to the subjects in my Bible study, *Preparing My Heart for Grandparenting*, also published by AMG Publishers.

The Bible study and this devotional book each stand alone. But if reading these devotions prompts a desire for a more in-depth biblical look at grandparenting roles, prayer, and passing on a godly legacy, you will find this in *Preparing My Heart for Grandparenting.*

Benefits for You and Your Grandchildren

I wrote this devotional book to bless you and your grand-children. At the end of each devotion, you will find a GRAND Thought (a key thought from the devotion) and a GRAND Response (your opportunity to choose ideas to build a deeper relationship with God and your grand-children). You may also decide to share the stories and GRAND Thoughts with your "joybringers." Or have fun to-gether in the kitchen making the recipes I've included with some of the devotions. You will also find space to record your thoughts and plans with each devotion.

Wherever you are in your grandparenting journey, let God direct you as you invest in the lives of your grandchildren. I pray God will use *GRAND Moments: Devotions Inspired by Grandkids* to give you many GRAND moments of your own. May God bless you and your grandchildren for gen-erations to come.

Happy grandparenting,

Lydia Harris (aka Grandma Tea)

Getting to Know You

Grandpa Milt and his first grandchild, Peter

Our Little Shepherd Boy

Young Peter dressed as a shepherd for Christmas

The Importance of a GRANDparent's Role

(Beyond spoiling grandkids and sending them home)

The devotions in this section relate to the topics in Week One of *Preparing My Heart for Grandparenting*, pages 1–31.

"Only be careful, and watch yourselves closely so that you do not forget the things your eyes have seen or let them fade from your heart as long as you live. Teach them to your children and to their children after them."

Deuteronomy 4:9

1. God's Lullaby

*He will take great delight in you. He will quiet you with
his love, He will rejoice over you with singing.*

Zephaniah 3:17 NIV 1984

Read: Zephaniah 3:14-17

The phone jarred me awake at two a.m. "We're going to
the hospital!" our daughter, Anita, announced. "The baby
is coming!"

The birth day of our first grandchild had finally arrived!
"Welcome to our world," the phrase from a familiar song,
played in my mind. I was eager to welcome this new little
one and make his world a warm, safe, and loving place.

I woke my husband, and we hurried to the hospital. (I
don't know why *we* were in such a hurry because the baby
wasn't.) As we waited, we prayed for a healthy child and a
safe delivery.

The ultrasound had revealed the gender, but I wanted
the official word before announcing our grandchild to the
world. After an eternity of waiting, a blurry-eyed new father came out and declared, "It's a boy! Peter is here."

When I saw our newborn grandson, it was love at first sight.
I cradled him in my arms, studied the shape of his cute

little nose, held his soft tiny hand, and thanked God for Peter Jonathan Faull. God had done it again. He had created another child in His image. "Lord, let Peter become a child of God too," I whispered in my heart.

After his birth, I delighted just to be with Peter. He didn't need to do anything special—just be himself. If he fussed, I cuddled him and soothed him with love and singing. My tender feelings toward Peter gave me a new understanding of a verse I held dear: "He will take great delight in you. He will quiet you with his love, He will rejoice over you with singing."

This verse assures me that God cherishes me, calms me with His love, and sings over me with joy. Imagine God feeling that way about you and me! As my heart overflowed with love for Peter and I treasured every moment with him, I gained a small glimpse of how much God loves me and rejoices over me.

Prayer: Oh, Lord, how precious it is to know You love me deeply and take great pleasure in me. Thank You for Your soothing love and tender mercies. I feel secure in Your love. Please help me to share Your tender love with my grandchildren.

GRAND Thought: God loves each grandchild and each of us with a deep, unending love. He delights in each one of us and rejoices over us with singing.

GRAND Response:

1. What can you do to show your grandchildren that you delight in them? Perhaps you could write them a note. Or post their photo or drawing in a visible place in your home. How can you help your grandchildren understand the ways God rejoices over them?

2. When our grandchildren were young, they enjoyed having me sing tender and sometimes silly songs that I made up about them. How can music enrich your time with your grandchildren? Think of songs you might share with them. You could write a song for each grandchild and sing it with them or to them.

3. Peter is now a young adult, and I am thankful for all the times we have shared. I often pray Zephaniah 3:17 for him and for all our grandchildren: that God will rejoice over them with singing, and that they will awaken each morning secure in our love and the marvelous love of their heavenly Father. What prayers or verses do you (or could you) pray for your grandchildren?

Your thoughts:

Grand Quotes:

"I love spending time with my grandparents. I would feel ripped off if I couldn't spend time with them." (Peter, age 10)

"What took me by surprise was the deep love I felt for my first grandchild. Now I have a better understanding of how deep and rich God's love is for me." (Grandma Bonnie)

2. *Basking in God's Love*

Give thanks to the LORD, for he is good;
his love endures forever.

Psalm 118:1

Read: Psalm 118:1-4, 19-29

I wanted to do something special for my grandson's second birthday. I decided to write short sentences about him, with a repeated refrain everyone could chant.

After Peter opened his gifts, it was time for the litany of love. I began, "Before the foundations of the earth, God planned for Peter's birth." Then everyone chimed in, "We love you, Peter, and we're glad you were born!"

Although Peter had his back toward us and was playing with his new toys, he turned when he heard the second chorus: "We love you, Peter, and we're glad you were born!" His grin widened as he listened. Soon he danced with glee as he heard the affirming words over and over. When we finished the last "We love you, Peter, and we're glad you were born!" he beamed and said, "Again!" Even a two-year-old can't get too much affirming love.

God knows we also need affirmations of His love. Psalm 118 repeatedly assures us that *"his love endures forever"* (vv. 1–4, 29). God's love is deep, and He demonstrates it beyond words. He answers us, and He is our salvation (v. 21). He does marvelous things (v. 23), saves us, grants us success (v. 25), and makes His light shine on us (v. 27).

Just as little Peter didn't tire of hearing our words of love, we can never receive too much of God's love. Experiencing God's love evokes our grateful response. Let's join the festive procession and worship the Lord (v. 27).

Prayer: Heavenly Father, "You are my God, and I will praise you; you are my God, and I will exalt you" (v. 28). Today, I bask in Your enduring love for my grandchildren and me.[1]

GRAND Thought: Nothing can ever separate us from God's amazing love.

GRAND Response:

1. How can you express love to your grandchildren? Jot down ideas of things you could do to help them feel loved. You might write a litany of love for each grandchild, perhaps for their birthday. See my litany for Peter as an example (Appendix, page 187). There are no wrong ways to do this. Say what suits you and your grandchild.

2. How can you help your grandchildren realize how much God loves them? How has God demonstrated His love toward you? List ideas and experiences you can share with your grandchildren, and thank God together for His great love.

---

1. Devotion adapted from *Preparing My Heart for Grandparenting*, pages 170–71.

Your thoughts:

Grand Quotes:

"My grandmother lived in Alaska, so I only met her five times in my life. But she was always sweet and kind. She never forgot birthdays or Christmas, and she made me feel special. I think of her with love and see her kind eyes and smile in my mind." (Grandma Bonnie)

"I grew up without grandparents living nearby. My husband and I wanted our children to grow up with grandparents involved in their lives so we moved back to our hometown. Our daughters spent quality time with their grandparents and great-grandparents, which enriched their lives. They did art projects, gardened, cooked, and sewed together. And Great Grandma taught them to play the piano." (Granddaughter Mary)

3. *Seize the Season!*

There is a time for everything, and a season for every activity under the heavens.

Ecclesiastes 3:1

Read: 1 Peter 2:2-3; 2 Peter 3:18

One October we invited Peter, age three, to our church's harvest carnival and for a sleepover afterward. He spent the evening jumping in inflatable bouncy houses and playing games where he earned candy prizes. On the way to our home, he fell asleep but awoke long enough to drag himself up the stairs and into bed. "I had so much fun," he said, then immediately returned to dreamland.

The next morning Peter said, "Let's go back!"

I hated to tell him, but . . . "The carnival is over."

"It was only for one day?" His face looked as sad as his voice sounded.

Looking into his disappointed eyes, I wished it were longer too.

Now, Peter has graduated from high school, and the season for sleepovers and bouncy inflatables is long past. Although I love the young man our grandson is becoming, sometimes I miss the little boy. I'm glad we shared childhood fun while we could.

Thankfully, I still have a few years to play with plastic dino-saurs and build forts with younger grandchildren. Too soon, I'll have to grow up and pack away childhood games. Then like Peter, I'll wonder, *Was it only for such a brief time?* My children grew up quickly, but it seems my grandchildren are growing up even more quickly! I need to seize the season today.

My grandkids' fleeting childhood reminds me of 1 Corin-thians 13:11: "When I was a child, I talked like a child, I thought like a child, I reasoned like a child. When I became a man, I put the ways of childhood behind me." In our phys-ical and in our spiritual life, God designed us to mature.

I don't ever want to grow up to the point of not having fun with my grandkids and future great-grandkids. But I do want to grow up spiritually and put away immature ways. In the scheme of eternity, when God looks at my life, I hope He sees my childish spiritual life as short—only a day. I want to keep maturing. "But grow in the grace and knowl-edge of our Lord and Savior Jesus Christ. To him be the glory both now and forever. Amen" (2 Peter 3:18).

Prayer: Heavenly Father, thank You for my dear grandchil-dren. Help me to make the most of the time I have with them and to model a growing faith in You.

GRAND Thought: God's plans and purposes for our lives include our spiritual growth. "Like newborn infants, long for the pure spiritual milk, that by it you may grow up into salvation (1 Peter 2:2 ESV).

GRAND Response:

1. How can you seize the moments and seasons with your grandchildren? What activities could you plan to do together? What special events that they participate in could you attend? For example, our grandkids appreciate our support at their church, sports, and music events. Afterwards, we take them and their family out for a snack or meal to spend time together.

2. As you interact with your grandchildren, how is God helping you to mature as a grandparent? For example, how are you growing in patience, understanding, acceptance, or other areas?

Your thoughts:

Grand Quotes:

"Nanas and papas see children very differently than mommies and daddies. We have seen how quickly a little one pulls his way up to wobbly knees, followed by toddling feet that all too soon make way for bicycle pedals. Babies are not babies for long. Toddlers are not toddlers for long. Children are not children for long." (Nana Colleen)

"My preschool-aged granddaughter enjoys playing with my tea timer with three colors of sand that flow through at different rates. The timer reminds me of the hourglass with the sands of life. Each grain represents moments of time. And eventually it runs out. The time with our grandchildren is limited." (Grandma Tea)

4. *Be the Grandma (or Grandpa) God Made You to Be*

In his grace, God has given us different gifts for doing certain things well. . . .

Therefore, accept each other just as Christ has accepted you so that God will be given glory.

Romans 12:6; 15:7 NLT

Read: Romans 12:3–8

Fridays are special because that's when four-year-old Anna comes to play with Grandpa and me. One time, as I prepared Anna's "caramel strawberries" for our little tea party, she said matter-of-factly, "My other grammy keeps her house cleaner than you do."

I giggled out loud. "Oh, I know!" I said. "Your grammy is very talented in housekeeping and keeps everything tidy. I love that about her." Then we sat down and sipped our peach tea with sugar cubes.

When I saw Anna's other grammy and poppy at church, I shared Anna's comment, and we all had a good laugh.

"I work full time," Grammy said, "so I have to stay on schedule and keep everything organized."

Although I majored in home economics and I've read many how-to books on organization, I haven't conquered clutter yet. Somehow, the organization gene passed me by. I'm learning to accept myself rather than compare myself to others, because the Bible says comparing is not wise (2 Corinthians 10:12).

After writing my first book, a friend sent me a note saying, "You're a celeb!"

I wrote back thanking her but clarified, "I'm a plain-Jane farm girl, and I like it that way." Her comment and my granddaughter's innocent remark got me thinking about being the person God created me to be instead of trying to become what others might expect of me. I wrote my thoughts this way:

Be the Grandma (or Grandpa) God Made You to Be

There are ritzy, glitzy grandmas
and homey, cozy ones.

There are busy, boisterous grandmas
and shy and quiet ones.

There are tall and slender grandmas
and short and stocky ones.

There are active, athletic grandmas
and relaxed and laid-back ones.

There are tidy, organized grandmas
And messy, cluttered ones.

There are funny, joking grandmas
and solemn, serious ones.

There are old-fashioned country grandmas
and modern city ones.

There are long-distance, faraway grandmas
and next-door-neighbor ones.

There are adopted and foster grandmas
and step-grandmothers too.

God gave you to your grandkids,
and gave these kids to you.

So whoever you are and whatever you do,
Just be yourself and celebrate you!

We're all different, and God planned it that way. In my grandparenting role, I want to grow in accepting myself just as Christ has accepted me (Romans 15:7). As I spend time with my grandchildren, their comments help me to understand myself and to embrace God's plan for my life.

Prayer: Thank You, heavenly Father, that I am one of a kind, and that's how You created me. I don't need to compare myself with others or to be like anyone else. Please help me to fully accept myself and glorify You with the strengths and abilities you have given me. In Jesus's name. Amen.

GRAND Thought: God made every person unique. It pleases Him when we accept our design rather than comparing ourselves to others and desiring their talents and qualities.

GRAND Response:

1. How are you uniquely suited to bless your grandchildren with your strengths and abilities? Think of times God helped you use your gifts when interacting with your grandkids.

2. How can you help your grandchildren accept and appreciate who they are? For example, if your grandchildren live close by, perhaps you can invite them over and share Anna's Favorite Caramel Strawberries. (See the recipe in the Appendix, p. 193.) As you chat together, discuss how God made each of us different and special according to His plan for our lives. The Bible says we are "fearfully and wonderfully made" (Psalm 139:14).

Your thoughts:

Grand Quotes:

"Our grandkids love us and think we are very special in spite of wrinkles, skin tags, and age spots." (Great-Grandma Sharon)

"A grandparent with a good ear for listening becomes a real friend for young ones. The grandchildren believe Grandpa and Grandma know what they're talking about and have been through it all." (Grandma Diana, missionary in Spain)

"We can't design the grandparents we want. We take what we get. And our love language influences what we want." (A grandmother)

5. **What Do You See?**

*But the L*ORD *said to Samuel, "Do not look on his appear-*
*ance or on the height of his stature. . . . For the L*ORD *sees*
not as man sees: man looks on the outward appearance,
*but the L*ORD *looks on the heart."*

1 Samuel 16:7 ESV

Read: 1 Samuel 16:1–13

My eyes focused on our nine-year-old grandson, Peter, as
the church's children's choir sang "Shepherd Boy." The
lyrics told the story from 1 Samuel 16 about how God looks
at the heart.

Samuel the prophet arrived at Jesse's home to anoint a new
king over Israel. Seven sons passed before the prophet, but
none were chosen. When Samuel asked if there were any
others, Jesse sent for his youngest son, David, probably an
adolescent, who was tending the sheep. Although young
and inexperienced, David was chosen and anointed as the
next king. The Bible says he was a man after God's own
heart (1 Samuel 13:14; Acts 13:22).

The story was familiar, but the song was new to me and
spoke to my heart. The thought that impacted me most
conveyed that although people may see just a shepherd,
God can see a future king.

I thought back to my childhood on a dairy farm—the
youngest of eight children. My siblings were attending

college or starting their careers, so I was the only one left at home to herd the cows into the barn for milking and to gather and clean chicken eggs for the market.

My eyes moistened as I recalled how God led me. I became a teacher, a mother, a leader in ministry, and—to my surprise—an author. Now, at age sixty-five, He had helped me complete my first book—a Bible study for grandparents. As the young choir repeated the chorus that people may see a shepherd when God sees a king, I replaced the words with, "When others see a farm girl, God may see an author."

The lyrics continued, explaining that our lives may seem commonplace, but God can touch us and change everything. Peter sang out like a young David. How did God see Peter? How should I see Peter and all the plans and purposes God might have for him?

Years later, this song still replays in my mind as I think about my grandchildren. Do I see the potential in them that God sees? How do you view your grandchildren? Do we see a colicky baby; a stubborn preschooler; a rebellious teen; a child with social, emotional, or physical problems? Or do we see a grandchild formed in God's image with tremendous possibilities? Someone whose life God can shape to fulfill His plans and purposes? My prayer is that I will see my grandchildren through God's eyes and from His perspective.

As Peter and the choir sang, I sensed the presence and power of the Holy Spirit. God would continue to direct Peter's life and mine.

Prayer: Dear Father, please give me Your view of each of my grandchildren. (Name each of them to personalize your prayer.) May I see their potential and partner with You to help them grow and mature. Like King David, may they and I become people after Your own heart.

GRAND Thought: God uses ordinary people to make an extraordinary impact. Although others may see only our grandchildren's outward appearance, God sees their hearts and the grand plans He has for each of them. That's what truly matters.

GRAND Response:

1. How do you view each of your grandchildren? Consider their strengths and potential. Ask God for eyes to see your grandchildren as He sees them.

2. How can you help your grandchildren develop spiritual qualities such as patience, self-control, and compassion? List ways to encourage and affirm them. For example, compliment your grandchildren for their efforts, accomplishments, and character development.

Note: You can find links online to the song, "Shepherd Boy."

Your thoughts:

Grand Quotes:

"Children are like flowers, beautiful when newborn, but they develop rapidly. An open flower is even more beautiful than the bud. I want to concentrate on their beautiful traits." (Grandma Sylvia)

"God speaks through grandchildren. It's a special moment when God speaks to our hearts through our own grandchild." (Grandma Tea)

6. *Sacrificial Love*

You see, at just the right time, when we were still power-less, Christ died for the ungodly.

Romans 5:6

Read: Romans 5:1-11

"How are you doing?" I asked my pregnant daughter when she called after her seven-month checkup. "Okay, I guess." Her voice sounded flat. She paused. "The doctor put me on bed rest so the baby won't come too early."

I sighed. That wasn't what I wanted to hear. We had prayed she would get through this pregnancy without the complications of the last one. With two-year-old Peter to care for, how could she rest? Although barely recovered from my own lengthy illness, I offered to help her. After all, she was my daughter, and I loved her.

I made the hour-long drive to her home several days each week to help with meals, housework, and caring for Peter. My own home chores remained undone while I completed hers. One day as I left her house, I said, "I'm investing in the life of my unborn grandson. Otherwise, he might not have a life."

Later, I realized that Christ did the same for us. He invested in our lives before we were born or born again so we could have abundant life on earth. But, more importantly, so we could have eternal life. "You see, at just the right time, when we were still powerless, Christ died for the ungodly" (Romans 5:6). Why did He die for us? To demonstrate His love for us (v. 8).

I made a small sacrifice of time and energy to help my daughter, who, after weeks on bed rest gave birth to a healthy son, our second grandchild, Alex. But Jesus made the supreme sacrifice by giving His life so we might live forever with Him.

Prayer: Thank You, Lord, for Your wonderful, sacrificial love. While I was an undeserving sinner, You died for me. Help me to demonstrate Your giving and forgiving love to others, especially to my children and grandchildren.[2]

GRAND Thought: Because of Jesus's death and resurrection, we have eternal life when we place our faith in Him. God wants us and our grandchildren to receive His gift of salvation and live with Him eternally.

GRAND Response:

1. How can you demonstrate self-sacrificing love to your children and grandchildren?

2. If your children or grandchildren have a current need, how can you help meet their need and show lovingkindness?

---

2. Devotion adapted from *Preparing My Heart for Grandparenting*, page 31.

Your thoughts:

Grand Quotes:

"We have life because Jesus gave up His life for us." (Grandma Tea)

As Clara (7) and I finished our tea lunch in a pleasant tearoom, I asked, "Which do you prefer? Going to tea or going to McDonald's?"

Her answer surprised me. "They're both about the same."

Well, I thought as I paid the bill, *then next time we'll go to McDonald's.*

A few months later, Clara and I made plans to go out together again. "Shall we go to McDonald's?" I asked, thinking that would cost less than afternoon tea.

"I think we should go for tea," Clara said. So as a grandma who lives up to her role and her title, we did. (Grandma Tea)

On Our Knees

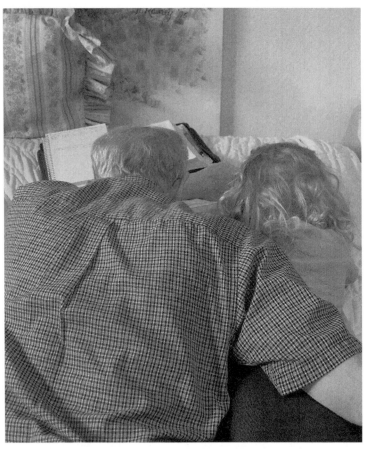

Grandpa Milt and his youngest grandchild, Anna,
kneeling in prayer

The Power of Praying for our GRANDchildren

(God answers knee-mail)

The devotions in this section relate to the topics in Week Two of *Preparing My Heart for Grandparenting*, pages 32–64.

7. Weaving Prayer into Our Grandchildren's Hearts

Before I formed you in the womb I knew you, before you were born I set you apart.

Jeremiah 1:5

Read: Psalm 139:13-16

When our daughter, Anita, announced they were expecting our first grandchild, my husband, Milt, immediately added this unborn child to his daily prayer list. When Milt and I prayed together that night, he said, "May this child become Your child, not just ours."

After Peter's birth, Anita recorded Grandpa Milt's prayer next to the scrapbooked photo of her newborn. She also added, "How blessed to have a praying grandpa."

God answered Milt's prayer. Peter accepted Christ as his Savior as a young child.

Since God is so intimately involved in forming our grandchildren in the womb, we can join Him by praying for them before their birth or even earlier. I know grandparents who began praying for their grandchildren when their children married. Others began even sooner—when their own children were born. I pray our current grandchildren and all future generations of our family will follow God with wholehearted devotion.

Besides praying for our grandchildren, it is precious to

pray *with* them. When our four-year-old granddaughter Clara was about to perform in a ballet, I went backstage to see the cute little bumblebee. She seemed excited and nervous. In the hubbub of other dancers, we hugged, and I prayed aloud that she would do a good job and not be afraid. After I said, "Amen," she added in a loud voice, "AMEN!" What a sweet moment we shared. (Although I do have a grandmotherly bias, the sixty-second flight of this bumblebee was fantastic!)

Prayer: Heavenly Father, thank You for the privilege of praying for and with my dear grandchildren. You know all about them because You knit them together according to Your plans. Make me a faithful prayer warrior, bringing my grandchildren to You often. Give me a prayerful heart, which responds to your prompts to pray. May I devote myself to praying for each of them each day.

GRAND Thought: Prayer makes a profound impact in our daily lives and for eternity. It is never too early or too late to begin praying for our grandchildren and encouraging them to pray.

GRAND Response:

1. What opportunities do you have to pray *for* your grandchildren? When could you also pray *with* them? Daily routines and special events can remind us to pray for them. For instance, every time we wash the dishes or laundry, we can pray for God to keep our grandchildren pure and to help them live holy lives. A doctor's appointment can

prompt us to pray for their health. A wedding urges us to pray for their future spouses and that God would bring the person He has for them into their lives at the right time.

2. See the Appendix on pages 182–185 for tips to pray for and with your grandchildren. Select and write down ideas you want to apply.

Your thoughts:

Grand Quotes:

"We are expecting our first grandchild! We're thrilled and already praying for this little life as God's knitting needles go to work!" (Grandma Gail)

Six-year-old Lena said: "When my family moved to Germany, I no longer lived near my grandparents. I missed praying with Grandma every morning."

"We took our three-year-old granddaughter Clara to see *The Nutcracker* ballet. When I told her *The Nutcracker* was about a girl named Clara, she said, 'Oh, I'm in it?!' Years later, she was—and played the Flower Fairy." (Grandma Tea)

8. *Good News!*

I will pour out my Spirit on your offspring, and my blessing on your descendants.

Isaiah 44:3

Read: Isaiah 44:1–8

One morning I received good news. Our young grandson had become a Christian!

The night before, Peter had asked what his Awana[3] memory verse meant: *"While we were still sinners, Christ died for us"* (Romans 5:8). His mother explained the verse and why Jesus died.

Peter's questions continued, and then he prayed, "Jesus, keep me safe. I want to go to heaven. I want to follow Jesus." After a moment, he confidently added, "Jesus will come and pick me up and take me to heaven."

His mother explained that would happen someday, but now he could follow Jesus by obeying the Bible. "If you want to follow Jesus, then you're a Christian," she said. "Are you a Christian?"

"Yes," Peter said.

She tucked him in, saying, "Good night, little Christian."

---

3. A Christian ministry in churches where children memorize Scripture verses and learn truths about God, Jesus, salvation, and the Bible. AWANA stands for Approved Workmen Are Not Ashamed.

He smiled and replied, "Good night, big Christian."

Months earlier, as I struggled with a serious illness with a bleak prognosis, I considered what could make the year special. My conclusion: our first grandchild's salvation. My husband and I had been praying for Peter's salvation since we first knew of his conception. God answered our prayers and poured out His blessing on our descendants (Isaiah 44:3). Now Peter could say, *"I belong to the LORD"* (v. 5).

When I told my husband, he shouted, "Hallelujah! Praise the Lord!" We celebrated with sparkling cider and thanked God for this wonderful answer to prayer. God, who formed Peter in the womb (v. 2), had poured out His Spirit on him. Now, we pray that Peter will become a strong witness for God.

Prayer: Lord God Almighty, thank You for the good news of salvation. Pour out Your Spirit, and use me to help my grandchildren and others find You as their personal Savior and to build a close relationship with you.[4]

GRAND Thought: We rejoice with the angels in heaven when God's Spirit draws our grandchildren to Himself and they accept Jesus as their Savior. What a thrill to know we will spend eternity together with the Lord!

GRAND Response:

1. Share with your grandchildren how you became a Christian. Also, tell them the difference God has made in your

---

4. Devotion adapted from *Preparing My Heart for Grandparenting*, pages 63–64.

life and how He continues to work in your life.

2. Consider ways to pass on your faith to your grandchildren—by your godly example, by sharing your life experiences, by inviting them to Christian events, and by praying with them.

Your thoughts:

Grand Quotes:

"My daughter wrote, 'Peter folded his hands when he got in his highchair. He again folded them when he saw us sit down to eat, even though he was playing nearby.' I hope Peter always has a heart for prayer." (Grandma Tea)

"I often share with my grandchildren what Jesus has done for me and the difference He has made in my life. I'm spontaneous in sharing His blessings." (Grandma Donna)

"I had prayed for my step-granddaughter's salvation throughout her life. After she became a grandmother herself, she came to visit me and asked many questions about God, Jesus, and the Bible. I explained as simply as I could. Then she said, 'I'm ready, Grandma.' You can imagine my thrill when God used me to lead her to Jesus!" (Great-Great-Grandma Shirley)

9. **Who Will Pray Now?**

*The prayer of a righteous person is
powerful and effective.*

James 5:16

Read: James 5:16-18

"Who will pray for me now?" our son, Jonathan, asked after he lost both grandparents within months when he was a teen.

His question startled me. He knew my husband and I prayed for him every day. But he also knew my parents had prayed aloud for him daily his whole life. If Jonathan had a French horn competition or challenging tests, they prayed—and he felt their prayers and God's answers. Now he sensed a loss, missing his grandparents and their prayer support. He wondered, *Will I be as successful without their prayers?* Indeed, who *would* pray for him now?

His question prompted me to join a Moms in Touch prayer group (now called Moms in Prayer), a group of moms who pray for their children and their schools. Perhaps our group's united prayers could replace his grandparents' powerful prayers. I also tucked my son's question away to ponder in my heart, knowing someday I might have grandchildren who would need my prayers.

God has blessed me with five grandchildren, and, yes, they do need my prayers. My husband and I pray for them

37

every day. I also pray weekly with other grandmothers, who follow the four-step format used by Moms in Prayer: praise, confession, thanksgiving, and intercession. Perhaps you've heard of it or a similar format with the acrostic ACTS (adoration, confession, thanksgiving, and supplication).

Before I joined this group, my prayers mostly consisted of a long list of requests. Learning this new method of prayer transformed my prayer life. Whether you're taking your first wobbly steps in prayer or have been skipping along with confidence for years, these four steps will strengthen your prayer time and bless your grandchildren. You can learn more about this pattern of prayer in the Appendix on pages 185–186.

Who will pray for *your* grandchildren? You will.

Prayer: Dear Father, thank You for the opportunity to pray for my grandchildren. Help me to consistently bring them to You. I know You hear and answer prayer, and I will give You thanks for Your work in my grandchildren's lives.

GRAND Thought: Our prayers make a powerful difference in our grandchildren's daily lives. They find comfort and security knowing we pray specifically for each of them and their needs.

GRAND Response:

1. Whenever you're with your grandchildren, watch for opportunities to pray with them or for them. And remember to share God's answers with them too.

2. Ask your grandchildren or their parents for specific prayer requests. Record them in a notebook. Also, record and date the answers to prayer next to the requests. You could make a separate journal for each grandchild. When it's full, give the notebook to your grandchild.

3. If you have a large family, you could draw a family tree with family names and use it to help you remember names and relationships as you pray for your children and grandchildren. Or perhaps you could use a card file with names and requests. I sometimes use a card file to record names of my grandchildren's teachers so I can pray for them.

Your thoughts:

Grand Quotes:

Great-Grandma Bobbi kept track of praying for her three children, eight grandchildren, and fifteen great-grandchildren this way: "I pray for them by family. I start with my oldest child and pray for his children and grandchildren. I pray for each one by name every day." Now she is in heaven, but her prayers live on, and her family continues to reap the rewards of her priceless prayers.

"One of the most rewarding things for me is seeing the values I instilled in my children lived out in my grandchildren. It shows me that the time I spent on my knees before the throne for my kids was time well spent." (Grandma Gloria)

Emily values her Grandmother Ruth's prayers and wrote to her: "We appreciated all of your prayers during my husband's job application process. He got the job! We are very excited about the opportunity this presents for his career. We would appreciate your continued prayers to help us navigate this next step."

10. *The Power of Praying Scripture*

*And Jesus grew in wisdom and stature,
and in favor with God and man.*

Luke 2:52

Read: Philippians 2:9-11

Throughout their school years, my children, Anita and Jonathan, appreciated my morning prayer sendoff before they left for school. If they were running late to catch the bus, they would hurry down the hall calling, "Pray, Mommy, pray." I was waiting at the top of the stairway: A hug, a short prayer, and they flew out the door.

When I began praying in a Moms in Prayer group, I learned how to pray using Scripture—praying God's Word back to Him for my children. As I read the Bible, I looked for verses I could pray for them.

One verse I continue to pray for my children and now my grandchildren is Luke 2:52. If Jesus grew in wisdom (intellectually) and in stature (physically) and in favor with God (spiritually) and people (relationally), I want my children and grandchildren to also develop mentally and physically and find favor in their relationships with God and others. As I pray for their growth in these areas, I sense God's peace and see His answers.

When Peter, our oldest grandson, was in the military and deployed to Europe, I longed for him to adapt well to his new environment and find favor with God and with others. As my husband and I prayed for Peter, God answered. Peter was honored with awards from two high-ranking generals for his significant work. Soon he graduated to the next rank and was praised for his diligence in serving above and beyond the bar. We rejoiced with him from a distance and thanked God that He answered our prayers so specifically.

Prayer: Dear Father, thank You for answered prayers. I'm grateful that You are always with my children and grandchildren even though I can't be. And when I pray, You hear and answer and meet their needs. Thank You for Your protection and blessings and for providing health and strength for my family. Thank You for my children's and grandchildren's growth intellectually, physically, spiritually, and relationally. In Jesus's name. Amen.

GRAND Thought: Praying God's Word for our grandchildren gives us a biblical focus, and it results in God-inspired prayers.

GRAND Response:

1. Ask God to give you verses to pray for your children and grandchildren. Examples of Scripture and character traits to pray for your grandchildren can be found in *Preparing My Heart for Grandparenting*, pages 46–48.

2. Use a passage such as Ephesians 1:16–19 or 3:14–19 to guide you as you pray that your grandchildren will grow in these spiritual attributes. Use their names and pray

specifically from the passage.

3. Pray with your grandchildren in person, over the telephone, or send them written prayers. They will learn to pray from your example.

Your thoughts:

.

Grand Quotes:

"After listening to her grandma pray all summer, Anna (four) almost always began her prayers with 'Dear heavenly Father' like her grandma. She also prayed regularly that her one-year-old brother would invite Jesus into his heart. He did when he was four." (Joan, mother of Anna)

Here's an example of how Papa Ron personalizes verses from Psalm 119 to pray for his three young grandchildren:

[1] "Blessed are Elton, Crosby, and Juniper as they make their way blameless, when they walk in the law of the LORD!

[2] Blessed are they when they keep your testimonies, as they seek you with their whole heart."

(He continues praying in this way through verse 8. Then he includes their names again as he prays for them from verses 9 through 16 this way.)

[9] "May Elton, Crosby, and Juniper keep their ways pure by guarding them according to Your Word.

[10] May they with their whole heart seek you; let them not wander from your commandments!

[11] May they store up Your Word in their hearts, so that they might not sin against you."

11. *The Gift of Prayer*

Thanks be to God for His indescribable gift!

2 Corinthians 9:15 NKJV

Read: Luke 2:8-20

"What do you like about Christmas?" I asked my six-year-old granddaughter Clara as we drove to a Christmas program.

"Presents!" she replied with enthusiasm and a giggle.

I could have squelched her response by saying, "Oh, but Jesus is the *best* gift." However, I didn't. I would have answered the same way at her age. Instead, we chatted about the American Girl doll she hoped to find under the Christmas tree. (And she did.)

Other times, I *have* shared with my grandkids how Jesus is the best gift of Christmas—God's indescribable gift. Together we've read the Christmas story of Jesus's birth from children's books and the Bible.

Presents are a special part of Christmas for grandkids and adults. Some peoples' love language is gifts, so they feel especially loved when they receive presents. Giving my grandkids gifts on their wish list is one way to express my love to them.

No matter their age or stage, I've found a gift where one size fits all—prayer! It's priceless, fits any budget, and outlasts other presents. It comes wrapped in love, tied with heartstrings, and yields eternal benefits. And no one will exchange this gift.

If you need a gift idea for Christmas or any time of year, consider the gift of prayer. Tips to give this gift follow this devotion.

Prayer: Dear Father, thank You for the indescribable gift of Your Son. Also, thank You for the priceless gift of prayer. We can come to You anytime, anywhere, and for any reason. You are always attentive to our prayers. Thank You for the comfort it brings to wrap my grandchildren in prayer, knowing You love them even more than I do. May I faithfully and consistently bless my grandchildren with prayer.

GRAND Thought: Prayer is the best gift we can give our grandchildren. It makes an eternal impact and outlasts any other gift. Our grandchildren will never outgrow their need for our prayers.

GRAND Response:

1. Read the "Tips for Giving the Gift of Prayer" that follow. Decide if you want to give a grandchild the gift of prayer and how you would do so.

2. *Preparing My Heart for Grandparenting* (pages 43–48) includes numerous scriptures to use when praying for your grandchildren as well as other ideas for meaningful prayer times.

Your thoughts:

Tips for Giving the Gift of Prayer

1. Ask God which grandchild or grandchildren especially need your prayers. If you have dozens of grandchildren, of course, you'll pray for all of them throughout the year. But do some need extra prayers? Does one grandchild have chronic health issues? Is an older grandchild in college? Is a grandchild struggling in some way? Give this special gift of prayer to only as many as you can faithfully pray for in this way.

2. After you decide who will receive this prayer gift, set aside a specific time when you will pray (e.g., weekly or as often as you have time). Will it be during your regular devotions or at another time? If you select a specific time and place, you're more apt to remain consistent.

3. With the gift of prayer, include a tangible gift to remind your grandchild of your prayers. For a young grandchild, the gift could be a cuddly teddy bear (prayer bear) with a note that says, "I'm praying for you." For an adult grandchild, consider a "prayer plant" with leaves that fold up at night like praying hands.

4. If you're married, it could be a joint gift from Grandpa and Grandma. My husband and I enjoy praying together for our grandchildren. Sometimes we also select specific scriptures to pray for them.

5. Ask your grandchildren or their parents for prayer requests or a favorite scripture passage to use during prayer. Keep a notebook with requests and answers. If you plan to give the notebook to your grandchild at the end of the year, make a separate notebook for each child for whom you're praying.

6. Expect to reap a harvest.

Grand Quotes:

"Before I had grandchildren, I began giving the gift of prayer to others. During my niece Ann's first year of teaching, I knew she would need prayer support. I committed to pray for her once a week for a year and gave her a prayer plant as a reminder. She sent me prayer requests, and God answered many prayers. It was a good year for her. Ann said, 'That's the best gift I could receive. I would like to receive it every year.'" (Aunt-Tea Lydia, aka Grandma Tea)

"During our summer family reunion, the oldest generation drew names of the youngest generation. They paired up to become prayer partners during the reunion and continued through Christmas, or longer if they wished. During that time, the grade-school age relative I prayed for became a Christian. Yes, God answers prayer." (Grandpa Milt)

"When we rely upon organization, we get what organization can do; when we rely upon education, we get what education can do; when we rely upon eloquence, we get what eloquence can do. And so on. But when we rely upon prayer, we get what God can do." (Dr. A. C. Dixon 19th century preacher and former pastor of Moody Church, Chicago, and Metropolitan Tabernacle, London, England)

12. *A Lifetime of Prayer*

Never stop praying.

1 Thessalonians 5:17 NLT

Read: Psalm 116:1-2

When our two-year-old grandson Peter stayed overnight, he crawled into bed with Milt and me for a short time before we tucked him into his own bed. As Milt and I took turns praying in short sentences, Peter looked back and forth at us, expecting the next one to pray when the other paused. A few times he joined in with a few words. How sweet to include Peter in our bedtime conversational prayers.

We may not realize it, but we're teaching our grandchildren about the importance of prayer. And they *need* our prayers.

Years ago, I wrote a poem to express my heart for prayer and to encourage mothers to continue praying for their children throughout their lifetime. Now I've adapted it for grandparents.

A Lifetime of Prayer
(for grandmothers and grandfathers)

As a new grandparent
I bowed in prayer,
"Lord, keep my dear grandchildren
In Your tender care."

With grandchildren in grade school
More fervent my prayers,
"Protect my dear grandchildren;
Remove all my cares."

A grandmother of teens
Intent on my knees,
"Lord, keep them from evil,"
More urgent my pleas.

With grandchildren in college,
New choices in view,
"Lord, guide their decisions.
Draw them closer to You."

A grandmother still faithful,
How soothing to pray,
"Lord, bless my grown grandkids,
Please, teach *them* to pray."

A gray-haired grandmother
Well-seasoned in prayer,
With confidence upholding
Generations in prayer.

A grandmother in heaven
One day I'll be,
Praising my Savior,
Who heard every plea.[5]

5. Adapted from Lydia's poem in *Preparing My Heart for Grandparenting*, page 193.

*"Let us then approach God's throne of
grace with confidence, so that we may
receive mercy and find grace to help us
in our time of need."* Hebrews 4:16

Not only do I want to model a lifetime of prayer, I also want
my grandchildren to begin praying at a young age and continue praying throughout their lifetimes.

Prayer: Dear Father, our grandchildren are so precious
to us, and we know they are even more precious to You.
No matter what stage of life we are in, and no matter what
trials or joys we face, please help us to make prayer a lifetime habit. We are confident that You hear and answer our
prayers, and we will reap the fruit of our prayers if we per-
severe in prayer. Draw us and our grandchildren close to
You every day. May we never stop praying. In the mighty
name of Jesus. Amen.

GRAND Thought: PRAY, PRAY, PRAY, and never stop!
"Pray without ceasing." God is always listening, and He
will answer in His perfect time and in His perfect way.

GRAND Response:

1. What ideas do you have to remind you to pray regularly
   for your grandchildren? You could set a time of day or
   during a certain activity to remind you to pray. For example, when you attend church on Sundays, pray for their
   salvation and spiritual growth. Or print the "Lifetime of
   Prayer" poem and keep it in a visible spot. If printed as

a bookmark, you could place it in your Bible or other books. Perhaps you could write out a reminder to pray for each grandchild and keep it in your Bible or put it on your mirror.

2. I think of prayer prompts as my GPS: Grandparent's Prayer Signal. Here are a few ideas I've used as my GPS to pray:

- I wear a bracelet, made by my granddaughter Anna, to remind me to pray for my grandchildren. With five grandchildren, I designate one weekday for each child.

- Granddaughter Clara and I planted daffodil bulbs and named them Claradils. When they sprout and bloom, they remind me to pray for Clara.

- Wearing the neck scarf I bought at the hospital when my grandson Owen had surgery helps me keep Owen close to my heart and prompts me to pray for him.

- As a preschooler, my grandson Peter made me a suncatcher. It's displayed in my kitchen window and reminds me to pray that the light of Jesus will shine through the lives of all my grandchildren.

Your thoughts:

Grand Quotes:

"Our values about prayer make a strong impression on our grandchildren. I want my grandchildren to learn positive aspects of prayer as they watch me." (Great-Grandma Barbara)

"When a Christian shuns fellowship with other Christians, the devil smiles. When he stops studying the Bible, the devil laughs. When he stops praying, the devil shouts for joy." (Corrie ten Boom)

When my grandson Jeff came home from preschool, his mother asked, "Did you have a nice day?"

"No," Jeff replied. "I knocked Massey down, and I feel so bad."

"Let's pray about it," his mother said.

"Oh no, don't tell God," Jeff said. "Then I'll really be in trouble." (Grandma Ruth)

The Significance of Modeling a Godly Life

(Not just as I say, but as I do)

The devotions in this section relate to the topics in Week Three of *Preparing My Heart for Grandparenting*, pages 65–99.

Arms Full of Love

Grandpa Milt and Grandma Tea with their grandchildren:
Alex Faull and Clara Harris
Anna and Owen Harris and Peter Faull

13. *That's Enough!*

Be kind and compassionate to one another, forgiving each other, just as in Christ God forgave you.

Ephesians 4:32

Read: 1 John 2:1-6

After waiting all week, Saturday finally arrived—a fun day for my husband, Milt, and me to spend with our grandsons, Peter, age six, and Alex, age four. That morning we cheered for Peter at his soccer game then shared lunch at McDonald's with the boys. Next up was The Frog Prince fairy tale at the garden center. When I checked my watch, I realized we would barely get to the play on time.

Just then Milt spotted a gas station with low prices and pulled in behind a line of cars, hoping we could still make it to the play before it started.

Getting gas took longer than expected. Milt became frustrated and pulled away from the pump before we were buckled in. My criticism of him started one of our "discussions." Although we kept our voices low, our grandsons sensed our tension. From the back seat Peter blurted out, "That's enough!"

Suddenly Milt realized he'd forgotten his five dollars change, but it was too late to return. Our cheap gas had become costly—in more ways than one.

After the play, once back at our home, our grandsons

romped in the colorful maple leaves, ate their favorite foods, played checkers, watched a movie, and snacked on cinnamon toast and hot chocolate. At eight p.m., two tired boys headed home with their parents. We'd had a big day!

As Milt and I recounted our fun memories, there was one part we wanted to forget. We realized our squabbling in the car had set a bad example for our grandsons. We apologized to each other and asked God to forgive us and help us model godly behavior.

The next time we saw our grandsons, I knew what needed to be done.

"Do you remember when Grandpa and I were fussing with each other in the car?" I asked.

"Yes," Peter said without hesitation. "I said, 'That's enough!'"

"We shouldn't have acted that way. Will you forgive us?"

Peter nodded and grinned. And that was enough, indeed!

Our behavior impacts our grandchildren. They watch us, learn from us, and copy us—whether good or bad. We are never off-duty. Even when we don't say a word, our actions speak volumes to our grandchildren.

Prayer: Dear Father, thank You that when we confess our sins You are faithful and just to forgive them (1 John 1:9). Please help us to admit our mistakes and quickly apologize to You and to our grandchildren. Also, may we be quick to forgive others.[6]

GRAND Thought: It's good to keep short accounts with God, our grandchildren, and others. Admitting our mistakes and asking forgiveness sets a positive example and keeps our relationships strong.

GRAND Response:

1. Ask God to show you if there are patterns of negative behavior you need to change in order to set a godly example for your grandchildren.

2. Is there someone you need to forgive or someone you should ask to forgive you? If so, set a possible time to do so. At times we may need to do this with a grandchild. After reconciling, we can pray together and share a hug.

Your thoughts:

---

6. Devotion adapted from *Preparing My Heart for Grandparenting*, page 65.

Grand Quotes:

"What I like about my grandparents is that they are generous, kind, and loving. I like to be around them." (Julia, age 10)

"As a grandmother of a preschool grandchild, I'm learning that teaching and leading by example don't end with parenting." (Grandma Wendy)

"My grandson, Logan, was part of the first-grade Sunday School class I taught. One of his friends in my class asked his mom, 'Is Logan's grandma God's mom? She knows so much.'" (Grandma Dianna)

14. *BIG Lips*

You should imitate me, just as I imitate Christ.
1 Corinthians 11:1 NLT

Read: 1 Timothy 4:9-16

One summer, when our grandsons Peter and Alex were grade-school age, they stayed with us for a week to attend our church's Vacation Bible School (VBS). This was a win-win situation for all of us. Grandpa and I enjoyed spending time with our grandsons, they had fun and learned more about Jesus, and their parents got a break.

One evening, as we got ready for a VBS event, I applied a touch of lipstick and eyebrow pencil.

Peter looked at me, frowning. "Grandma, your eyebrows go up, and your lips are big."

I laughed, curious about his remark. "Do I look better without makeup?"

Peter nodded.

Later, I felt God speaking to my heart, *If he notices simple things like makeup, what else do you think he's noticing?*

That made me stop and think.

The apostle Paul makes this bold statement, "You should imitate me, just as I imitate Christ" (1 Corinthians 11:1 NLT). I'd like to shorten the verse to say, "Imitate Christ." I'm not confident I could always say, "Imitate *me*" to my grandchildren. After all, sometimes my example isn't something I would want my grandchildren to follow.

I do, however, want to model 1 Timothy 4:12 (NLT), "Be an example to all believers in what you say, in the way you live, in your love, your faith, and your purity." Through my words and deeds, I desire to show them my faith is alive.

Paul doesn't leave us without instructions. He shares how to set an example that is worthy to follow. "Whatever you have learned or received or heard from me, or seen in me—put it into practice. And the God of peace will be with you" (Philippians 4:9).

Our grandkids are always watching us. They notice every little detail, whether BIG lips or BIG love. Or . . . BIG mistakes. When I fall short, I can ask God and my grandchildren for BIG forgiveness.

Prayer: Dear Father, I long to set a godly example for my grandchildren to follow. Please forgive me when I fall short. I pray my words and actions will reflect Your love and bring glory to Your name. "May the words of my mouth and the meditation of my heart be pleasing to you, O LORD, my rock and my redeemer" (Psalm 19:14 NLT).

GRAND Thought: Our grandchildren watch our behavior and learn how to live the Christian life by what we say and especially by what we do.

GRAND Response:

1. How has God helped you to set a godly example through your speech and actions?

2. What examples of behavior that please God could you share with your grandchildren? What behaviors have you noticed your grandchildren copying by watching you?

3. Memorize a verse together, such as Psalm 119:11. "I have hidden your word in my heart that I might not sin against you."

Your thoughts:

Grand Quotes:

"Our grandkids make me laugh. When our grandson Owen was a preschooler, he was eating a cookie with frosting. He smeared some of the frosting on his lips and said, 'I have 'kissy lips.' When I kissed him, I got frosting on my lips. Owen laughed and repeated this for another sweet kiss!" (Grandma Tea)

"What I like about Grandpa Bill and Grandma Ruth is that they are always willing to listen to me. They are models in every way." (Andrew, age 11)

"Grandchildren watch what we say and do. They can see that church and Sunday school are important to us." (Grandpa Bill)

15. *Coloring Outside the Lines*

God made him who had no sin to be sin for us,
so that in him we might become the righteousness of God.

2 Corinthians 5:21

Read: Colossians 3:1-4

"Let's put mine in front," my five-year-old granddaughter, Anna, said. She pointed at a picture of a teapot, cream and sugar, and cup and saucer. Her older sister, Clara, had colored this masterpiece for me when she was about eight, and I framed it and displayed it in my dining room. When Anna was nearly four, she colored an identical picture and gave it to me.

Her request was easily done since I rotate my grandchildren's art. As I opened the back of the frame and placed Anna's picture in front of Clara's, she studied her work. "I could probably do better now."

"Yes, now you're older," I said. "But I like your picture with all the pretty colors."

Anna grinned, seemingly pleased with my affirmation. I returned her smile, happy to display her art.

To some, Anna's coloring might look like messy scribbling not worth displaying. Yet, colored when she was not yet four, Anna had done her best to color inside the lines. I treasure her beautiful gift of love as well as the artist who created it.

Perhaps that is how God sees me. In my Christian walk, I certainly don't always stay perfectly inside the boundary lines of His commands. At times, my attitude about life gets messy. Because Jesus died for my sins and I have placed my faith in Him, God doesn't see me and my mistakes. Instead, He sees me as righteous *in Christ*—His perfect Son.

As I grow and mature spiritually, like Anna I might say, "I can do better now." Old things are gone, and I am a new person in Christ. "For you died, and your life is now hidden with Christ in God" (Colossians 3:3).

Jesus changed places with me, and now He's in front. When God looks at me through the lens of Jesus, He sees me as beautiful. I am in Christ, and I am treasured and loved.

Just as I felt pleased with Anna's imperfect picture because she is my grandchild, I know God smiles when He sees imperfect me—His child—now righteous in Christ Jesus.

"See what great love the Father has lavished on us, that we should be called children of God! And that is what we are!" (1 John 3:1).

Prayer: Heavenly Father, thank You for making a way for me to be part of Your eternal family. I love being a child of God. Help me model a godly life for my grandchildren so they are drawn to Jesus.

GRAND Thought: God loves us even though we're not perfect. When He looks at those who have placed their faith in Him, He sees Christ, His beloved Son, the perfect One.

GRAND Response:

1. Coloring has become popular with adults, and there are lovely illustrated Bible verses to color. Perhaps you can color with your grandchildren. As you do, how can you demonstrate God's love and share it with your grandchildren? In what other ways can you show them God loves them, no matter what?

2. Think of simple things your grandchildren did that pleased you, and thank them. Is there something they made that you can display to affirm them? If so, why not surprise them and show it off to others?

Your thoughts:

Grand Quotes:

"Knowing that I am 'in Christ' is very precious to me. It reassures me that I have an eternal future with God. The song 'In Christ Alone,' is one of my favorites. You can find numerous recordings of the song online and could share it with your grandchildren." (Grandma Tea)

"Memories aren't just something for old people. Kids love them too. And if you don't create them now, what will you have later?" (Grandma Nancy)

16. **Who's the Winner?**

Let each of you look not only to his own interests, but also to the interests of others.

Philippians 2:4 ESV

Read: Philippians 2:1–11

Our granddaughter Anna bounded into our home carrying a bouquet of flowers she had picked from her yard. "Happy Mother's Day," she said, even though the holiday was a few days away.

Anna, nearly six, had arrived for an afternoon of fun. I needed to test a recipe for a children's magazine, so we headed to the kitchen for a finger-lickin' good time. As I got out the ingredients to make Chocolate Pudding Cones, I realized you can't go wrong with a recipe made with chocolate pudding, Oreo® Cookies, whipped cream, M&M'S®, and marshmallows.

Anna did a good job of crushing the cookies to become "dirt crumbs" to go into the ice-cream-cone "flowerpots." She planted an M&M® "seed" in the flowerpot. Then we filled the cone with pudding, and she sprinkled chocolate cookie dirt on top.

Next, we made a flower from a marshmallow so the seed could sprout into a pretty posy growing on top. I took Anna's picture with her culinary creation. And then came the best part—eating the pudding cone, dirt and all.

We still had time for more fun and games, so Grandpa and Anna headed downstairs to play air hockey. As they hit the puck back and forth, Anna kept scoring. So, she gave Grandpa tips to improve his game. "You have to block the goal," she said. "Don't let me win." Still, Anna kept her winning streak.

After that, Anna wanted to play a boxed game she enjoys—Hullabaloo. She and Grandpa followed the recorded instructions and stepped from one colored shape to another. As the game ended, they both landed on the same square, which turned out to be the winning one. They were both winners. Of course, I already knew that.

The afternoon whizzed by, and soon it was time to take Anna home. I sent pudding and cones along with her so she could make a treat for her family.

The next morning, I asked Milt, "Did you let Anna win on purpose?"

"Yes," he replied, just as I suspected.

"Why?" I asked.

"There's no need for me to win," he explained. "She's more important."

Since Anna and Grandpa were both rooting for the other to win, they were modeling Philippians 2:4, which says we are not to think only of our own interests but also to consider the interests of others.

And with a husband and granddaughter like that, *I'm* the real winner!

Prayer: Heavenly Father, thank You for the joy of grandchildren and the sweet example Anna and Milt set as they played together. And thank You for loving us and for setting the greatest example of humility and putting others first. Help me to grow in following You and considering the interests of others above my own. In Jesus's name. Amen.

GRAND Thought: God is pleased when we follow His example and place others, including our grandchildren, before ourselves.

GRAND Response:

1. As grandparents, how can we model putting others first? If letting kids occasionally win a game isn't something you would do, how else could you model putting your grandchildren first?

2. God knows how to sweeten our days. How can we sweeten the lives of our grandchildren with our attitudes and actions?

For a sweet treat, you will find the recipe for Chocolate Pudding Cones in the Appendix on pages 199–201.

Your thoughts:

Grand Quote:

When my son, Peter, was young, he asked me, "Mom, who is your grandma?"

"My grandmas don't live here anymore," I replied. "Grandma Siemens was one of my grandmas. She lives in heaven with Jesus."

"I miss your grandma," Peter said. "I have two grandmas. Grandma Tea and Grandma Faull are my grandmas. I'll share my grandmas with you, Mom." (Anita, Peter's mom)

17. *What Motivates You?*

Jesus said to them, "My food is to do the will of him who sent me and to accomplish his work."

John 4:34 ESV

Read: John 4:31–38

"Would you like to help me make apple strudel?" I asked my three-year-old granddaughter, Anna.

"I'd rather watch the movie," she replied, cuddled in the playroom with her cousins for their New Year's Eve sleepover. "But I'd like to taste what you make."

"That's fine." I chuckled and was reminded of the Little Red Hen, whose friends wouldn't help make the bread but were happy to help eat the baked bread.

In the kitchen, I prepared the ingredients for the strudel then returned to Anna, knowing she would enjoy helping. "Would you like to help me paint with butter and sprinkle on sugar?"

"Sure," she said, running ahead of me to the kitchen.

What made the difference? Anna loves to paint and likes sugar.

This made me stop to think about what motivates me—especially if a task isn't appealing or might be a challenge. If I could choose between housework and watching a movie, like Anna, I would probably choose the movie.

Unless …

Unless I have a motivation stronger than my own comfort. I consider, in a positive way, that my days are numbered, and I can choose to spend them in a meaningful way.

At this season of life and grandparenting, the words of Jesus in John 4:34 are a strong motivation for me. I want to follow His example of doing God's will and accomplishing His work for me. I have the model of Jesus, who had thirty-three years on earth to accomplish God's purpose. God sent Jesus to pay the penalty for our sins and to redeem us. And He did.

As a young child not much older than Anna, I accepted His free gift of eternal life. Now, as a grandmother, I long for my grandchildren to know Jesus as their Savior. My greatest desire is for all my grandchildren, present and future, to accept Jesus so we can all be together in heaven forever.

Prayer: Dear Father, may my life reflect the sweetness of Your love and draw my grandchildren close to Jesus. I pray all generations from now until Christ's return will follow You with wholehearted devotion and accomplish Your purposes for their lives.

GRAND Thought: Following Jesus's example of doing God's will and accomplishing His work not only pleases God. It blesses our present grandchildren and all future generations!

GRAND Response:

1. What motivates you in your spiritual life? How can you pass this incentive on to your grandchildren?

2. What is your deepest desire for your children and grandchildren? How can you guide them toward this goal?

Your thoughts:

Grand Quotes:

"When our oldest grandson turned twelve, my husband took over as his chief grand mentor. Each week they would meet and go through a portion of the Christian book *Boyhood and Beyond* by Bob Schultz, which was written to encourage boys to become men of God." (Grandma Val)

"When our first grandson was two, our children were not attending church regularly. We picked up our grandson and took him to Sunday school. After a while, he began asking his parents to take him, and they did." (Grandma Carole)

"The greatest lesson I learned from my own children also applies to my grandchildren. They aren't mine. They belong to God. I am here to serve Him and He is the one who does the work in them and makes the big decisions about life and death." (Grandma Bonnie)

(See the Appendix, pp. 194–195, for our family's Apple Strudel recipe.)

18. **Don't Shut the Door**

Here I am! I stand at the door and knock. If anyone hears my voice and opens the door, I will come in and eat with that person, and they with me.

Revelation 3:20

Read: Revelation 3:20-22

Our five-year-old grandson, Owen, grinned as he bounded up the stairs, ready for fun at our home. As usual, he brought something to play with—this time a box of BAND-AIDs®.

"Do you want to be the doctor?" I asked.

He nodded.

"Grandpa will be your patient tonight, and you can stick BAND-AID®s on his arms," I said. "Grandma needs to work in her office, so I'll shut my door to keep it quiet. But if you need something, you can come in." My book manuscript was due the next morning, so I couldn't join the fun as usual.

Owen smiled and ran down the hall to play with Grandpa.

Soon the door opened, and Owen handed me a piece of typing paper and plastic scissors. "I need this cut into long hair," he said. I cut the paper into strips and taped strands of "hair" to the back of his shirt collar. Satisfied, he ran off. I shut the door and began writing again.

About ten minutes later, Owen peeked in and said, "I'm

hungry." We headed to the kitchen and made his favorite snack. As he nibbled his flour tortilla with melted cheese and chatted with Grandpa, I returned to my office and closed the door.

Within minutes, Owen poked his head in again. I wondered what he wanted this time.

"Don't shut the door," he said with a sweet but imploring voice. His words touched my heart as I realized Owen didn't want to be cut off from me. He wanted a relationship with me. I left the door open the rest of the evening.

And just that quickly, God whispered to my heart, *Lydia, I don't want you to shut Me out of your life either. Always leave the door of your heart open for Me. My door is always open for you, because I want an ongoing relationship with you.*

I felt convicted as I recalled the times I had closed the door on God. Sometimes I was too busy to spend time praying and reading His Word. Other times my work competed with my relationship with Him, and I focused on immediate matters, neglecting more important spiritual priorities. Owen taught me a valuable lesson: to leave the door of my heart wide open—for God and for my grandkids.

Prayer: Oh, Father, thank You for reminding me of Your desire for an open-door relationship with me. Please forgive me for the times I've been too busy or distracted to include You. I'm grateful You always have time for me and welcome me into Your presence. I'm blessed to be Your child. In Jesus's name, I pray. Amen.

GRAND Thought: God is never too busy to spend time with us. He is eager to develop a close relationship with us. When we come near to God, He will come near to us (James 4:8).

GRAND Response:

1. How can you show your grandchildren the door of your heart is wide open for them? Perhaps you could invite them over for a special event or one-on-one time, plan outings with them, take a trip together, take time to listen when you're together, or write to them. What other ideas do you have?

2. How can you encourage your grandchildren to open their heart's door to Jesus? (See pp. 179–181 to share the Path to Salvation.)

Your thoughts:

Grand Quotes:

"My grandmother was blind, so she never saw me. But when I visited, I sat on her lap and we rocked and sang 'The Old Rugged Cross' and 'Amazing Grace.' I didn't attend church as a child, so this was my church. I learned Bible truths from these hymns. It was wonderful." (Dianna, now a great-grandmother herself, with an open heart and home for her grandchildren and others)

"Since our daughter and family live in their RV on our property, most mornings our two young grandsons come over. Often, I build a fire in the firepit and sit watching the sun come up with a little guy in my lap. One morning I told my young grandson, Elton, I had taught his mom how to build things when she was young. He wanted to make a cup holder for my coffee mug. We cut wood scraps to size, and I showed him how to drill holes and screw the wood together, which he did with pride. His brother made one too. We created a "papa moment" for both of them. It's a privilege to spend time with my grandchildren and teach them skills." (Papa Ron)

19. *A Rock-Solid Foundation*

*Therefore everyone who hears these words of mine and
puts them into practice is like a wise man who built his
house on the rock.*

Matthew 7:24

Read: Matthew 7:24–29

"Another song," a sweet little voice begged from the back
seat of the car. While driving our two-year-old granddaughter Clara home, my husband and I sang one Christian chorus after another. She enjoyed the words and the motions,
and sometimes she chimed in. As we sang, "The wise man
built his house upon the rock," we paused to let her fill in
words like *rock, sand,* and *crash.*

Singing Christian choruses with Clara made our travel
time joyful and allowed us to plant seeds of spiritual truth
in her life. But it also made me pause to consider how to
apply the lessons from the wise man so I would become a
wise woman.

According to Matthew 7, what does that mean? Building
a house on a rock foundation is preferable to building
on sand. And everyone wants a home that will withstand
winds, storms, and rain. But these verses are not about
building a physical home. They are about building a life
on Jesus, the solid Rock. And when we do, God considers
us wise, and we set a good example for our grandchildren.

But how can we know if we're building wisely? According to Matthew 7:24, wise builders not only hear God's words, they also act on them. Their foundation is firm. But those who don't apply God's Word are like foolish carpenters, building on shifting sand.

Today, I need to dig deeper and evaluate my life's foundation. Does it pass God's building code for a solid base? When the floods of adversity beat on me, I want my grandchildren to notice through my life that the house on the Rock stands firm.

Prayer: O Lord, You are my Rock, my firm Foundation. I want to build my life on You alone. Help me to model a godly life for my grandchildren, so they also want to build their lives only on You.[7]

GRAND Thought: Jesus Christ is the only solid foundation for my life and my grandchildren's lives.

GRAND Response:

1. If you have young grandchildren, you could teach them "The Wise Man" song and sing it together with motions. (https://www.youtube.com/watch?v=zAjEjxX-DhA.)

2. For older grandchildren, draw pictures to go with Matthew 7:24, or build something together with LEGOS® or building blocks.

---

7. Devotion adapted from *Preparing My Heart for Grandparenting,* pages 98–99.

3. At the beach, play in the sand and demonstrate a sandy foundation.

4. With older grandchildren: discuss examples of strong and sandy foundations in life. How would you picture or describe a strong foundation and a shaky one? Why is Jesus Christ the only sure foundation?

Your thoughts:

Grand Quotes:

"Sometimes I sang songs with my children at bedtime, including 'The Wise Man,' where the last verse says, 'So build your life on the Lord Jesus Christ.'

One evening when I tucked my preschool-age daughter into bed, her eyes lit up with a revelation. 'I know why we can't see Jesus. We built our life on Him!' " (Grandma Sharon)

"I will not run my life, because when you add *I* to run, it becomes ruin." (Grandma Tea)

"At age two-and-one-half, Clara was our travel reporter. Often, she gave us a running commentary of what she saw when we rode in the car together. As we passed a tarp-covered pile of dirt, she called out, 'Look at the dirt.' Then she added, 'They keep it covered so it won't get dirty.' " (Grandma Tea)

The Privilege of Investing in Our GRANDchildren's Lives

(Love Is Spelled T-I-M-E)

The devotions in this section relate to the topics in Week Four of *Preparing My Heart for Grandparenting*, pages 100–135.

Making Seasons Bright

Grandma Tea baking cookies with Owen, Anna,
and Clara Harris

20. *Hold Me*

How precious is your steadfast love, O God! All people
may take refuge in the shadow of your wings.

Psalm 36:7 NRSVA

Read: Psalm 36:5–10

When my husband, Milt, and I were grand-sitting our two
grandchildren, Milt played pretend games with two-and-a-
half-year-old Clara. Meanwhile, I tried to keep two-month-
old Owen happy by holding him and rocking him. When
their mom returned a few hours later, I handed Owen to
her. Clara immediately looked up at me and asked, "Do you
want to hold me?"

I didn't hesitate a moment. I scooped Clara into my arms
and hugged her. Then I sat and bounced her on my lap
and hugged her some more. Clara had waited hours for my
attention, and I was happy to assure her of my love in ways
she understood.

In Psalm 36, David paints a picture of a God who knows
our needs and who delights in loving us, His children, in
tangible ways. But we don't need to wait for our turn. God
can love each person in the whole world at once!

God's steadfast love is so immeasurable, it extends to the
heavens (v. 5). Because He loves us, He provides a protec-
tive place of refuge under His wings (v. 7) and supplies an
abundant feast and drink from His river of delights (v. 8).

He also gives us life and light (v. 9) and offers us righteousness and salvation (v. 10).

When we come to God with our needs, we don't need to question His love and ask, "Do You want to hold me?" God's Word assures us of His limitless, steadfast, precious love that extends far beyond anything we can ever comprehend.

Prayer: O Lord, Your steadfast love is precious to me. Thank You for providing a refuge for my grandchildren and me in your loving arms.[8]

GRAND Thought: God is always eager to hold us and comfort us. "The eternal God is your refuge, and underneath are the everlasting arms" (Deuteronomy 33:27).

GRAND Response:

1. What makes your grandchildren feel loved? In their book, *The 5 Love Languages of Children: The Secret to Loving Children Effectively,* Gary Chapman and Ross Campbell discuss these five ways to show love: quality time, affirmation, service, gifts, and physical touch. When you're with your grandchildren, notice which type of love they respond to most.

2. List your grandchildren's names with their love languages to help you remember and plan how to best meet their needs for love. Look for ways to express love to them

8. Devotion adapted from *Preparing My Heart for Grandparenting,* pages 134–135.

in their love languages. For example, if their love language is service, offer assistance when they need it. If it's affirmation, watch for opportunities to praise them.

Your thoughts:

Grand Quotes:

"I hope you like my present," nine-year-old Clara said looking at me in anticipation. Inside the wrapping paper, I found an illustrated handwritten booklet titled, "Why I Like Grandma Tea." I gave her a big hug.

"Thank you, Clara!" How could she fathom my love language was words of affirmation? "I'll read it later," I continued. "If I read it now, I'll cry." And ten years later, her special gift still touches my heart. (Grandma Tea)

"Our son's love language is service, so Milt and I showed our love by helping him take down their family's Christmas lights. But the love came full circle as I shared moments with our 'joybringers' after we finished our part. How blessed to hear our youngest grandchild smack her lips and say 'hot shocklat' as we shared a snack. And to find our six-year-old grandson hiding in the bushes and pretending to be a dinosaur. Also, to comfort my oldest granddaughter as she again showed me the marker in their yard to remember the golden retriever they recently lost. We gave a little time but received much more." (Grandma Tea)

21. *Grandparenting One-on-One*

My brothers and sisters, practice your faith in our glorious Lord Jesus Christ by not favoring one person over another.

James 2:1 GW

Read James 2:1-5, 8-10

We were grand-sitting Anna when her siblings Clara (eight) and Owen (six) arrived home from school. Since Clara and I sometimes meet for spiritual sharing, she asked, "Grandma, when are we getting together again?"

"I'll talk to your mom and set a date."

Coincidentally, while we were there, our daughter, Anita, called to finalize plans for Grandpa and me to spend time with her two sons. First, a birthday brunch at an extra-special restaurant to honor the new teenager, Peter. Then a special activity with his younger brother, Alex.

Owen overheard my conversations about spending time with Peter, Alex, and Clara, and he plopped down beside me on the couch. I gave him a hug as he reached for the calendar and looked at me.

I knew what he wanted. "Shall I put you on my calendar too?" I asked.

Owen nodded.

"How about Friday? You don't have kindergarten that day."

"When is that?"

"Day after tomorrow," I said. "Would you like to go to the Creation Station to build something? And go for a treat?"

"What about going to the toy store?" He asked with a smile.

Two days later, when Papa (as Owen calls Grandpa) and I arrived to pick up Owen, he had his bag packed: LEGOS®, green-lizard Bible, his Awana book, pencils, and paper.

We started with ice cream cones and then the Creation Station, where Owen discovered bins full of carpet samples, felt, stickers, tubes, and all sorts of pieces and parts to make thingamajigs. With Papa's help, he created several things, including an airplane. That became his new toy.

When we took Owen home, Clara reminded me, "Sunday we're getting together for our special time."

Milt and I feel blessed that our five grandkids live nearby. Although we get together with all of them at once for cousin time, we also treasure giving them each individual attention. We quickly learned that our grandkids want equal treatment. None want to be left out. No favorites.

The Bible includes many verses that say God opposes favoritism. He favors everyone. And with our grandchildren, that's our goal as well.

We've never taken a class in Grandparenting 101, but we've learned the value of grandparenting one-on-one with each grandchild. This builds relationships and helps them feel special.

Prayer: Dear Father, thank You for each of my grandchildren. Please make me sensitive to their individual needs. Alert me if I'm overlooking any or showing favoritism in any way. I want to follow Your example and love them impartially and unconditionally. By my words and actions, may I show equal love, favor, and acceptance to each of my grandchildren.

GRAND Thought: God loves every person equally. He designed each of our grandchildren with unique talents and personalities, and He wants us to treat each grandchild without partiality.

GRAND Response:

1. What plans can you make to spend individual time with each of your grandchildren? What are their individual interests? How can you help them pursue these interests?

2. Ask God to help you show love and acceptance to each child according to his or her age and interests.

3. To keep it fair and help you remember whose turn it is, you could use a calendar to record the dates you spend with each grandchild. Later you can look at the calendar together and talk about the times you shared. Also, take pictures when you're together so you can share photo memories later.

Your thoughts:

Grand Quotes:

"When I'm with the grandchildren, I'm not too busy to spend time with them. I let them take turns staying overnight so they get one-on-one time with me." (Grandma Dot)

"Must I dust? Or should I play? What would make a happy day?

For me . . . for my grandchild?

Lord, help me balance work and play, to make a happy day

for my grandchild and me." (Grandma Tea)

"When I was a child, I thought Grandpa and Grandma came to town to visit me. It seemed like they spent their whole time with me—talking, telling stories, and going on walks. When they worked in the yard, they always let me help them and made it seem like fun. It wasn't until much later that I realized they also came to see my parents." (Granddaughter Joan)

22. *Falling into Fun*

*Charge them . . . to set their hopes on . . . God, who richly
provides us with everything to enjoy.*

1 Timothy 6:17 ESV

Read: Psalm 67

"This was so much fun," my granddaughter, Clara, said as
she got ready to leave our home.

"What made it fun?" I asked.

"Jumping into the leaves and making huckleberry pancakes," she replied.

I reflected on the day. We had enjoyed a simple, unscripted
Sunday afternoon with Clara and Owen. We raked colorful
maple leaves into a pile, and the kids ran down the sloping
front yard and jumped into them.

"I'm going to jump into the leaves too," I said.

"You are?" Owen asked eyes wide.

"Why not?" After all, who says a grandmother can't enjoy
playing?

After the fun in the fall leaves, Clara suggested, "Let's go
to the backyard." Surprisingly, we still found huckleberries
on the bushes and began eating them.

"Do you ever make huckleberry pie from these?" Clara
asked.

"There aren't enough left for a pie," I said. "Should we make huckleberry pancakes?"

"Yes!" they both agreed.

Grandpa joined in the fun of cooking with us. He helped mix the pancake batter and stirred the homemade maple-flavored syrup.

Soon the huckleberry pancakes were cooked, and we all sat down to enjoy a tasty treat.

Later, while Owen and Grandpa played with dinosaurs and fabric pumpkins, Clara and I worked on a craft project. We chatted about squirrels and how they stored nuts for the winter. I mentioned that the Bible tells us to store God's Word in our hearts. "I have stored up your word in my heart, that I might not sin against you" (Psalm 119:11 ESV). As a reminder, I gave her a squirrel pin to wear on her coat.

I love these spontaneous occasions with our grandkids. Milt and I feel great satisfaction when we all create happy memories together.

These experiences remind me that we can have spontaneous times with God as well. He loves to encourage us through His Word and gently guide us by His Holy Spirit. Sometimes He may whisper a spiritual truth to my heart, and other times He surprises me with tangible gifts, leaving happy memories. Whether it's November or any season of the year, God provides richly, giving us so much to enjoy.

Prayer: Thank You, Lord, for all the beautiful and fun things we receive from Your gracious hand each day. In Jesus's name. Amen.

GRAND Thought: All good gifts come from God, who loves to bless and delight His children (James 1:17).

GRAND Response:

1. Recall a fun time with your grandchildren and thank God for it.

2. What activities or events can you plan to enjoy with young grandchildren? Could you take them to a playground, a park, or the library? Or prepare a treat together, enjoy a picnic, play a favorite game, or teach them a skill.

3. For an older grandchild, consider attending a special event together or sharing a meal in a restaurant or in your home. Or help your grandchild complete a project.

See the Appendix for the recipes for Perfect Pancakes (p. 212) and Homemade Maple-Flavored Syrup (p. 208).

Your thoughts:

Grand Quotes:

Clara, our young granddaughter, was finishing her breakfast when Grandma and I stopped by for a visit. As she ate the last bites of cereal, we discussed our favorite breakfast foods.

"Do you like pancakes?" I asked.

"Yes," she replied.

"Do you eat them with syrup?"

Clara looked puzzled. "No, I eat them with a fork."

(Papa Milt)

While I took a walk with my five-year-old granddaughter, I pointed to the tree ahead and said, "I'll race you to the tree."

She looked at me with big eyes and said, "I didn't know grandmas could run."

I raced her to the tree, and we tied! Now she knows. (Great-Grandma Dianna)

23. *"I Love You, Grandma"*

Grandchildren are the crown of the aged.

Proverbs 17:6 ESV

Read: Psalm 128

"I love you, Grandma," three-year-old Anna said in her sweet little voice.

I smiled and replied, "I love *you*, Anna," and hugged her. This became our frequent greeting.

Then one day Anna changed the familiar pattern and said, "I love you, Anna." We giggled, and I replied, "I love you, Grandma." That started our little game of reversing our words of endearment. But whether I'm called Anna or Grandma, the loving bond remains.

Often, I start the dialogue. If I don't, Anna will. One day, as she sat in her car seat and we said our goodbyes, she smiled and said with a tease, "I love you, Anna." (I wish you could hear her voice when she says these words.)

But Anna isn't the only grandchild with whom we've used sweet words or an affectionate title. "You're my little sweetheart," I used to tell my grandson Peter when he was three. Later his mom told me, "Peter says he's your sweetheart."

When Peter became a teenager, my ways to show him love changed. Though I used to invite him for sleepovers and take him to playgrounds, as a teen he was happy to receive a batch of his favorite cookies or a package of smokehouse bacon, which he fried up himself.

Using endearing language can become a fun tradition, and hopefully a habit. The words may change, but the sentiment never does. This verbally tells our grandkids what we think of them and how much we love them.

The second Sunday in September is Grandparents Day—which is to honor grandparents. It's also the perfect time to love and affirm our grandkids. But we don't need a holiday to spend time with them, think about them, or invest in their lives.

If you're blessed with grandchildren, one of the most powerful ways to impact their lives is to pray for them. If possible, connect in other ways as well—such as in person, by email, phone, texting, video meets, sending a letter or card, or any way that expresses, "I love you."

Each of my five grandchildren holds a special place in my heart. I'm glad God put us together in families (Psalm 68:6). We need each other. I treasure them. They are my crown. Grandchildren indeed are the crown of the aged (Proverbs 17:6).

Prayer: Thank You, Lord, for the gift of family and grandchildren. Show me ways to love and affirm them. Work in my heart and through my life so my words and actions build up my grandkids and draw them to You. Thank You for the privilege of investing in their lives.

GRAND Thought: Welcoming our grandchildren into our lives and homes will bless them and us now and continue into the future.

GRAND Response:

1. There's nothing like the hugs and kisses we give and receive from our young grandchildren. Ask God to show you precious moments where you can make your grandchildren feel completely loved.

2. In school, young children often bring their favorite belongings for "show and tell." As grandparents, how can we "show and tell" our grandchildren how special they are to us?

3. How can we grow in our relationship with our grandchildren? *Preparing My Heart for Grandparenting* includes a chart with ideas from A to Z to affirm grandchildren (pages 112–114).

For example, **A** includes, "Accept each child as a unique individual created in God's image." **P** reminds us, "Pray for them daily—without fail." **Z** says, "Zero in on ways to make them feel loved and to help them reach their potential." A scripture verse accompanies each affirming action.

Your thoughts:

Grand Quotes:

"When my granddaughter was expecting her first baby, she posted the ultrasound picture on Facebook. My response was, 'I love this little one already.' She wrote back, 'It loves its great-grandma already too! I can feel it.'" (Grandma Donna)

"While our son and his wife went away for their anniversary, both sets of grandparents shared the joy of watching the grandkids. When it was time to return the 'joybringers,' both grandparents' cars arrived at the same time. Clara jumped out of their car and ran toward us. 'It's a party!' she said. 'Both sets of grandparents are here!' Her spontaneous excitement thrilled us. We couldn't have received a nicer compliment. Yes, families are an important part of God's plan (Psalm 68:6)." (Papa Milt and Grandma Tea)

24. *My Huckleberry Friend*

But Jesus said, "Let the children come to me. Don't stop them! For the Kingdom of Heaven belongs to those who are like these children."

Matthew 19:14 NLT

Read: Matthew 19:13-15

"Chick-a-dee-dee, chick-a-dee-dee," my five-year-old grandson Owen repeated as he mimicked the bird chirping outside our kitchen window.

"What kind of bird is that?" I asked Owen. "Is it a chickadee?" I hadn't heard the bird's song until Owen echoed it.

Owen and I sat at the kitchen table making tart shells to fill with "huckles," as he calls huckleberries. With his hands deep in the bowl, mixing flour and butter, he continued, "Chick-a-dee-dee, chick-a-dee-dee," smiling as the words rolled off his tongue. After the dough was mixed, we rolled out the crust and formed tart shells to bake. With all the flour on his apron, I considered baking it too.

Then we headed outdoors to pick huckles for the tart filling. After picking only a handful, Owen said, "I think that's enough." Off he ran to check the apple trees for fruit while I kept picking berries. Fortunately, I had pre-picked several cups of berries before he came.

Soon he reported, "No apples," then surveyed my berry stash before helping me pick a few more.

Owen chattered when we went inside to wash and sugar the huckles. "Yummm," he said as he sampled the sweet but tart berries. While the berries simmered, we whipped the cream. Of course, Owen licked the sweet cream off the beaters.

Eager to sample our tasty treat, we filled the baked tart shells with fruit and topped them with whipped cream. After Owen ate some, he licked his fingers and gave me a blue huckleberry smile. I packaged the remaining tart shells, huckleberry sauce, and whipped cream for Owen to share with his family.

Before Owen came, I had debated whether I had time for him that day. I needed to finish preparing my grandparenting talk to present in a few days. Later, I realized spending time with Owen was the perfect preparation. After all, there's nothing like the lessons a five-year-old can teach. I learned:

1. Listen for the birds and enjoy their songs.

2. Put your all into life and get some flour on your apron.

3. Savor every lick of whipped cream.

4. Take time for the little (and big) people in your life.

But mostly, I learned to take time to invest in my grandkids' lives while I can—because kindergartners don't keep. They turn into young adults almost overnight. I'm thankful I made time for Owen that day.

Prayer: Thank You, Lord, for the lessons we learn from our grandchildren. Just as You always have time for me, help me to make time for my grandchildren.

GRAND Thought: Jesus made time for children and welcomed them. It's a privilege to spend time with our grandchildren and build a relationship with them.

GRAND Response:

1. What do your grandchildren enjoy doing? Do they enjoy sports, art, music, swimming, board games, or reading? How can you come alongside them and do things together that interest them?

2. What have you learned from your grandchildren? What can you teach them?

You will find the recipe for the Huckleberry/Blueberry Tarts in the Appendix on pages 206–207.

Your thoughts:

Grand Quotes:

"The grandchildren 'season' will soon seem as short as the huckleberry season. Take time to make memories with them now." (Grandma Sylvia)

"Grandparenting is a second chance to impact our children's lives and to build bonds of love. To love the grandkids is to love the parents." (Grandma Petey)

"When my young granddaughter comes over, I drop everything to play with her. I follow her around the house and indulge her wishes. She likes to pretend she's taking a bath and plays with her toys in the tub. Her short visits allow me more playtime than when I was managing so many responsibilities as a mom." (Grandma Wendy)

25. *Join Their Fan Club*

Therefore encourage one another and build each other up, just as in fact you are doing.

1 Thessalonians 5:11

Read: 1 Thessalonians 2:6–13

Our grandchildren and their parents enjoyed watching *American Idol*, where contestants competed in vocal music. A young man from our area had returned home as the winning contestant.

Although my husband and I didn't watch that program, our kids and grandkids had faithfully followed the singer and were attending his homecoming. On the spur of the moment, we decided to meet our family at this welcome-home event.

Crowds lined the streets, and noise and excitement filled the hot summer air. We found our clan and chatted as we waited for our hometown hero. Fans chanted the winner's name and anticipated his arrival. Finally, a car with the local celebrity drove down the main street. People waved signs and cheered.

After he passed by, I turned to our grandkids and said, "Everyone came to see the winner. But we came to see *you*."

My oldest grandson, Peter, said, "But Grandma! I can't sing like that."

"It doesn't matter," I said. "You don't need to sing. We love you just as you are, and we like to spend time with you."

I'm not sure he understood. But, no matter what, Grandpa and Grandma are co-presidents of his fan club, and we'll cheer him on through life.

Now, years later, this grandson has grown up and joined the military in his early twenties. We cheered him on with letters, packages, and our ongoing prayers. When he came to town on leave, we hosted a family gathering to spend time with him and pray with him. When he was deployed and distant, our prayers intensified.

No doubt, the family of the winning singer was thrilled and proud of their son. We're happy for them. We're also proud of our grandson as we watch God shape Peter into the hero He wants him to be.

God has plans for each of our grandchildren. Whatever they are, we can join their fan clubs, pray for them, and cheer them on . . . and on . . . and on.

Prayer: Dear Father, thank You for my grandchildren. I know You have plans for each one. Help me cheer them on at each stage of life. As they mature in age, may they also grow in their faith in You.[9]

---

9. Adapted from pages 120–122 in *Preparing My Heart for Grandparenting.*

GRAND Thought: Grandparents can make a dramatic difference as they recognize and affirm their grandchildren's gifts and help them reach their potential.

GRAND Response:

1. Each child has different talents. If one child is strong in chess, then play chess with him or her. If one likes to build sand castles, start there in the sand. Guide your adult children to help their children (your grandchildren) find and develop their God-given talents. Then support them as they do.

2. Show up for your grandchildren—at games, school, concerts, and other events. They don't have to be stars. Show interest in whatever they enjoy doing and encourage them.

3. Every grandchild needs fans to cheer them on. My Bible study, *Preparing My Heart for Grandparenting,* shares how to join their FAN club and become their **F**riend, **A**ffirmer, and **N**urturer (pages 108–122).

Your thoughts:

Grand Quotes:

"My grandson, Hiroto, mastered the Rubik's Cube® in record time. I asked him to help me master the cube. With Hiroto's skill and help, I only completed the top and the middle layers, but it brought us together." (Grandma Val)

"When grandkids are older, they have less time for grandparents. But their earlier memories of time we shared draw them back to us because of the love relationship we established." (Grandma Gail)

"From our grandson in the military, deployed to Europe: 'Thank you for sending the package. Your gift really brightened my day. Even though this is my first Christmas away from home, the gifts and packages the family has been sending me have made me feel like I'm not too far from home after all.'" (Grandpa and Grandma Tea)

26. *How Do You Spell Love?*

And now these three remain: faith, hope and love.
But the greatest of these is love.

1 Corinthians 13:13

Read: 1 Corinthians 13:4–13

One Valentine's Day weekend, while our son and his wife celebrated their wedding anniversary, Milt and I had the pleasure of grand sitting their three young sweethearts, ages four to eleven. I planned food and fun with a "heart-y" theme to make our time special.

We started by drawing names so we could show extra love to the person whose name we drew. Then we made valentines for each other from colored construction paper, doilies, and stickers. My four-year-old granddaughter, Anna, took her valentine-making seriously. She kept whispering to her older siblings and Papa (as they call Grandpa) to get the information she needed. I wondered what she was up to.

Next, we each made our own valentine holders from stiff paper plates and hung them from our dining room chairs.

The heart theme continued with heart-shaped pizza for dinner. The next morning, we had breakfast with waffles cut into hearts and topped with whipped cream and heart-shaped strawberry slices. We sipped hot chocolate from heart-shaped teacups and added a dollop of whipped cream and pink sprinkles.

After breakfast, we looked into our cardholders and read our valentines. When I opened mine from Anna, I found crooked strips of colored construction paper with letters printed on them. Stringing the pieces together, I discovered they included the entire alphabet. Anna smiled up at me expectantly, as if she knew I would love her note. I smiled back and thanked her with a big hug.

Anna couldn't write words and messages, so she simply wrote all the letters of the alphabet so I could create my own words. Now I had endless possibilities for loving messages—and the greatest of these is love.

I still cherish those jagged scraps of paper—because to me they *really do* spell L-O-V-E.

As much as I cherish Anna's love, God's love is far greater. God's Word is filled with letters, stories, and words that spell LOVE.

Prayer: Dear Father, thank You for Your deep and vast love. You love me with unconditional, never-ending love. You are patient and kind, and Your love never fails. Help me express Your amazing love to my grandchildren in every season, not only on Valentine's Day. I pray in the name of Jesus, the name above all names. Amen.

GRAND Thought: God has poured His love into our hearts, so it can flow through us to our children, grandchildren, and others (Romans 5:5).

GRAND Response:

1. First Corinthians 13 includes sixteen characteristics of love. You could make paper chains with your grandchildren with one characteristic written on each loop. Give each grandchild a chain as a reminder of how to love others. You could mail chains to your grandchildren who live farther away. Keep a chain for yourself too. Stay linked together as you each remove and read one link a day and put that characteristic into practice.

2. One Valentine's Day, I sent this short message of love to my grandchildren. Maybe you could write your own.

   Let
   Others go first.
   Be **V**ery kind to
   Everyone.

3. Read verses from the Bible about God's love to your grandchildren. Or write them a note about love, or tell them a story that demonstrates how someone showed love to you.

Your thoughts:

Grand Quotes:

"If you show your grandchildren genuine love, you will have a tremendous influence for good in their lives. Teach them lessons you've learned from the Bible, and they'll have a better compass to make decisions." (Grandpa Bill)

"I don't regret a minute I've spent with my grandchildren." (Grandma Erna)

"My son and his wife seemingly couldn't have a baby, so they adopted a baby girl from China. A China doll! Later they did have a son. But they also adopted another girl and then a boy from China to complete their family. The last two adopted children had the same congenital heart condition and needed surgery. Both are doing well now. Oh, how I love each one of them!" (Grandma Juli)

Celebrating Joy and Tears

(It's Not All Fun and Games)

The devotions in this section relate to the topics in Week Five of *Preparing My Heart for Grandparenting*, pages 136–171.

Our Cup Runs Over:
Celebrating 50 Years of Marriage

Celebrating God's faithfulness with our children and grandchildren:
Center: Grandpa and Grandma Tea
Back left: Amy, Clara, and Jon Harris
Right side: Steve, Alex, Anita, and Peter Faull
Front Center: Owen and Anna Harris

27. Anna's Fun Day!

I will sing the Lord's praises, for he has been good to me.

Psalm 13:6

Read: Psalm 13

"Remember what day it is?" five-year-old Anna asked. Her blonde curls bounced as she bounded up the stairs, excited to spend the day with Grandpa and me. Before I could answer, she declared, "It's Funday!"

We had previously coined "Funday" to mean any day we spend with our grandkids. So, although it was Friday, today was "Funday."

To begin, we decided to go out for a tea lunch. (No cooking or cleanup for Grandma, and Grandpa enjoys tea outings too.)

"This is the best lunch ever," Anna said as she ate her crustless turkey and raspberry-cream-cheese sandwich with gusto. And instead of tea in her dainty teacup, she sipped hot chocolate. All three of us had a deliciously fun time.

On the way home, we stopped to buy flowers and ingredients to make cookies for her parents' "sweet sixteen" anniversary that day.

Anna got right into mixing the flour, softened butter, and cream with her hands. When the delicate dough was mixed, we rolled it out and cut several sizes of heart-shaped cookies. Then Anna and Grandpa dipped the cookies into sugar and placed them on a cookie sheet.

While we worked together, Anna startled me by saying, "I have a hard life."

"Why is that?" I asked.

She lamented about being the youngest in the family and that her older brother picked on her. "I wish I weren't the youngest."

"God planned for you to be the youngest," I explained and hugged her. "Grandpa and I are so glad you were born into our family." I also mentioned how blessed she was with so many who loved her—friends, family, grandparents, and God. "Some children don't even have a home or parents," I said, hoping to change her perspective. As she licked the sugar from her fingers, I thought, *Surely, her life is sweet, not hard.*

After the cookies were baked and frosted, we set up a little tea party at our dining room table with peach herbal tea and heart-shaped cream wafers we had baked and filled with pink and purple frosting. Anna looked at me with a wide grin and proclaimed, "This is the best day of my life!"

"I'm glad," I said, hoping I really had changed her perception about having a hard life.

Soon she added with enthusiasm, "I have lots of best days."

Later, when Anna's dad picked her up, she took home the flowers, cookies, and the "Anna"versary card she had made for her parents with a large, red, heart-shaped doily and lots of stickers.

Yes, it really had been a fun day—for her and us!

Later, I thought about her "hard life" comment that turned into the "best day" statement. It reminded me of King David's words in the Book of Psalms. Sometimes he began a psalm with a woe-is-me attitude. But by the end, he had a definite change of perspective and praised God for His goodness, as in Psalm 13.

Looking at my life, I realize how easy it is to dwell on difficulties instead of trusting God and focusing on the good He provides. I determined, whether my grandkids come to visit or not, with God's help and my heart tuned to praise Him, every day can be Funday!

Prayer: Dear God, thank You for Your great love for my grandchildren and me. You add such joy and sweetness to our everyday lives. Remind me to look for Your goodness even during hardships. I want to praise You whether I experience struggles or smiles. I praise You that You're always with me, and I rejoice that You are the one and only true, living God. And You are *my* God. Thank you. Thank you!

GRAND Thought: It's a joy to know Jesus and grow to trust Him more. We can choose to praise God and find joy, even when our circumstances are difficult.

GRAND Response:

1. Have you experienced a "hard life?" How has God changed your perspective during difficult seasons? Ask God to help you praise him amidst your difficulties.

2. How can you help your grandchildren see God's goodness during the hard times of life? Share examples with them of how God has helped you.

3. For a sweet time, bake the Melt-in-Your-Mouth Cream Wafers with your grandchildren. See the recipe in the Appendix on pages 209–211.

Your thoughts:

Grand Quotes:

"When our grandchildren know we are experiencing a difficult period in life, it's good for them to see and hear that we are still filled with joy and thankfulness toward God." (Grandma Val)

"In my hard experiences, ultimately, I've found that God works in everything for my good—whether He builds my character or makes me value someone or something more. That's how my perfect Father has worked in my life. I'd like to approach all trials with that in mind first." (Grandma Felicity)

"As I've grown older, God has reminded me to put Him first. When I do, the Holy Spirit, our Comforter, brings me joy and peace and shows me ways to bring joy to others. That's how God changes my perspective on life." (Great-Grandma Barbara)

28. *Expecting Joy*

*For the joy set before him he endured the cross,
scorning its shame, and sat down at the right hand
of the throne of God.*

Hebrews 12:2

Read: Hebrews 12:1–3

"More coupons, please," two-and-a-half-year-old Owen said with a smile. We laughed at our spunky grandson and were happy to give him what he really wanted—salad *croutons*. Owen's family and his four grandparents had gathered to celebrate the one-year anniversary of his successful open-heart surgery.

While we sat in the restaurant, my mind flashed back to a year earlier when we first learned our seventeen-month-old grandson needed his heart repaired. I remembered the surgeon's grim words as I accompanied our son and his wife to the appointment. "We'll stop his heart and put him on a heart-and-lung machine." I sat motionless, troubled by a question I couldn't speak. *What if he dies?*

That night, I cried myself to sleep. When I awoke the next morning, I found a damp pillow and tears still running down my cheeks.

I longed to shield my son, Jon, Owen's dad, and his family from this stress and uncertainty. I told Jon, "I feel so terrible that you have to go through this scary time."

But God never abandoned us during this trial, and He gave me hope. One morning before Owen's surgery, I awoke with this verse of Scripture on my mind: "For the joy that was set before Him, He endured the cross." I knew the words came from the Bible, and I searched until I found them in Hebrews 12:2. I felt certain God's Spirit had placed this passage in my thoughts to encourage me.

As I reflected on the verse, I realized that while Jesus awaited the cross and endured the pain of crucifixion, He set His mind on the joy to come—when He would conquer sin and bring salvation. I sensed God wanted me to focus on the joy ahead while I endured the grief and unknown outcome of the upcoming surgery. So, whenever I thought of Owen's surgery, I fast-forwarded to the joy that would come when his heart was healed—either on earth or in heaven.

Now, a year later, I looked at our rosy-cheeked, energetic grandson—the toddler who did not have enough energy to crawl before his surgery. I thanked God that Owen could now run, talk, and loved to pray. When the meal to celebrate his recovery ended, Owen and his four-year-old sister sang a Sunday School chorus, "Hosanna to the King of Kings." In my heart, I sang hosannas with them. God certainly had replaced our sorrow with joy and praise.

Owen is seventeen now and loves God. We still sing praises to the King of kings.

Prayer: Dear Father, thank You that You are with me in all circumstances. I can call on You anytime to help me endure hardships and trust You for future joys. Thank You for Christ's selfless example of enduring suffering and dying on the cross to save us from sin and bring healing. I praise You for Your love and grace.

GRAND Thought: God is with us during our times of fear and uncertainty. He encourages us in our trials with His presence and His Word, which give us hope and comfort.

GRAND Response:

1. You may not have a grandchild who has experienced a serious illness or surgery, but you have probably faced other trials with your grandchildren. How has God helped you through these difficult times?

2. How is God working in your life right now? Write a prayer of petition or thanksgiving, according to your current needs.

Your thoughts:

Grand Quotes:

When our grandson read the story I had written about his heart surgery, he began to cry. "I could have died," he said.

"I'm sorry I had you read a sad story," I said.

"No," he replied, "you touched my heart." (Grandma Tea)

"I think the most difficult thing as a grandparent is trying to surrender my grandchildren to the Lord. I am not their parent. I cannot 'fix' their folks. But I take great comfort in the way God preserved my children in spite of my mistakes and character flaws, and I must trust He is willing to do so with my grandchildren." (Grandma Debbie)

"My grandson, Logan, was born nine weeks early with under-developed lungs and had difficulty breathing. His mother said, 'Pray that he survives.' Logan remained in the hospital for nine weeks and then came home on oxygen. God answered our prayers for his survival, and Logan became a healthy, rambunctious toddler that got into everything. Then his mother requested, 'Pray that *I* survive *him*!' Now Logan is married and expecting his first child." (Great-Grandma Dianna)

"Happiness is based on chance. Joy is based on choice. It's my choice to rejoice." (from a message given by Pastor John Czech, June 2009, Northshore Baptist Church)

29. *A Gift from God*

Children are a gift from the LORD;
they are a reward from him.

Psalm 127:3 NLT

Read: Psalm 127:3-5

Our grandson Peter's eighth birthday was approaching. I wanted to bless him and affirm God's work in his life. After reading Psalm 127 in my devotions, I prayed and thanked God for Peter, our gift from God. Then I wrote this chant, to be read in rap rhythm, at his family party. Together we repeated, "Peter is a gift from God!"

Peter Is a Gift from God

The phone awoke us in the middle of the night,
PETER is a gift from God!
Announcing that Peter would soon be in sight.
PETER is a gift from God!

What a joy to meet our special grandson,
PETER is a gift from God!
When we first saw him, our hearts he won.
PETER is a gift from God!

He's happy, outgoing, and friendly to all;
PETER is a gift from God!
To new people he says, "Hi! I'm Peter Faull."
PETER is a gift from God!

He grew and grew and developed so fine;
PETER is a gift from God!
We've watched him play soccer in rain or shine.
PETER is a gift from God!

He's creative on paper and in the sod,
PETER is a gift from God.
He planted a garden and grew pea pods.
PETER is a gift from God!

At three, Jesus came to live in his heart,
PETER is a gift from God!
He studies his Awana and does his part.
PETER is a gift from God!

In school he does great in reading and math,
PETER is a gift from God!
He has a tender heart and walks in God's path.
PETER is a gift from God!

We just can't believe he's already eight,
PETER is a gift from God!
To describe him we say, "He's terrific and great!"
PETER is a gift from God!

We're all so thankful for the boy God made,
PETER is a gift from God!
God gave us even more than for what we prayed.
PETER is a gift from God!

We pray for many blessings throughout his life,
Because PETER JONATHAN FAULL is a gift from God!

After we finished reciting our poem for Peter, we prayed together for him and hugged him. Then it was time for gifts and birthday cake. As Peter opened his gifts, we already knew he was *our* best gift that day.

Afterwards, I gave Peter a letter that included his poem and this prayer:

Dear Peter,

After I read Psalm 127 in my devotions, I gave thanks for you, our gift from God, and wrote the poem in honor of your eighth birthday.

Lord, we pray that Peter will be a solid ROCK like Peter in the Bible. And may he be like Jonathan in the Bible, who was a kind, caring friend to David, the future king of Israel. Thank You, Lord, for the gift of Peter.

Love,

Grandpa and Grandma Tea

Prayer: Thank You, Lord, for the gift of children and grand-children. Surround my grandchildren with Your love, protection, and blessings. Help me to treasure them as a reward from You, which they *truly* are. May Your favor rest upon them as You guide them throughout their lives.

GRAND Thought: Our grandchildren are cherished by God and are His precious gifts to us.

GRAND Response:

1. Find a favorite Scripture verse or passage. Read it prayerfully, and ask God to help you use it to write a loving, affirming note to your grandchildren. It could be for a special occasion or any time. Remind them often how precious they are to you and to God. For another example of a birthday poem, see "A Birthday Ode for Owen" in the Appendix on pages 189–190.

2. Write your grandchild's name vertically and select an affirming word or Bible verse to go with each letter of the name. Sometimes we do this spontaneously while traveling in the car with them. For example: ANNA.

A is for affectionate
N is for nice
N is for neat
A is for artistic

Other times we may use different words for the letters to affirm her.

Your thoughts:

Grand Quotes:

"When we select gifts for others, we give intentionally and thoughtfully—and so does God! My grandchildren are a gift from God. He knows what they need, and He chose me to be their grandmother." (Grandma Val)

"At our grandson's fourth birthday party, his mother said, 'I want Owen to open this present first.' Inside Owen found a shirt that said, 'I'm going to be a big brother.' We all cheered and clapped! The next morning Owen asked his mother, 'Where's the baby?'" (Grandma Tea)

30. *Blackberry Promises*

*Know therefore that the L*ORD *your God is God;*
he is the faithful God, keeping his covenant of love
to a thousand generations of those who love him and keep
his commandments.

Deuteronomy 7:9

Read: 1 Corinthians 4:1-5

Our grandson Alex loves blackberry pie. You might even say it's his "love language." When Alex and his older brother, Peter, came for a sleepover, I asked, "Would you like me to bake you a blackberry pie to take home?"

"Yes!" Alex exclaimed. Peter offered to help. But, before we began mixing the piecrust, the phone rang.

"We had a cancellation, so your husband can see the doctor this morning," the receptionist said. This was an answer to prayer. Relieved, I took the appointment.

"I'm sorry we can't bake a pie after all," I told the boys. "I need to take Grandpa to the doctor." Although disappointed, they didn't complain. "Maybe another time," I said.

Days later, as I began writing a Bible study lesson on faithfulness, I felt God nudge me to surprise the boys with a blackberry pie. I would see them soon at a family birthday party. Perhaps this was the "another time" I had promised them.

By the morning of the party, I was rushing to meet a writing deadline. I didn't have time to bake a pie. Or did I? What a dilemma—bake a pie for my grandsons or write.

When my grandsons arrived at the party, I said, "Alex, I have a surprise for you." When he saw the pie, he beamed and thanked me, then proudly carried the pie to his parents' car.

God's Word says, "The one who is faithful in a very little thing is faithful also in much" (Luke 16:10 NASB). I'm not sure if baking the pie was a little thing or a big thing. What *we* think is insignificant and what *God* considers important may differ. But I felt it was important to keep my word to my grandsons and model following through on promises.

Faithfulness is evident in our lives when we fulfill our vows, promises, and agreements. "When you make a vow to God, do not delay to fulfill it" (Ecclesiastes 5:4).

We also model faithfulness when we finish assignments. Paul the apostle writes in 1 Corinthians 4:2: "Now it is required that those who have been given a trust must prove faithful."

I'm glad God helped me finish the writing assignment and also gave me an opportunity to demonstrate faithfulness by baking a pie for my grandsons. Blackberry smiles are the best.

Prayer: Heavenly Father, thank You for Your example of faithfulness. I can always count on You because You never go back on Your Word. Please help me grow in modeling a faithful example for my grandchildren and others.

GRAND Thought: God is always faithful, and He is pleased when we keep our word. If we follow His example, one day we will hear Him say, "Well done, good and *faithful* servant!" (Matthew 25:21, emphasis added).

GRAND Response:

1. Recall a time when you experienced God's faithfulness. Record your experience. When you have the opportunity, tell your grandchildren about it (face-to-face, in writing, or at a virtual meetup online).

2. What is your grandchild's favorite food? Perhaps you could make it with or for them. See the recipe for Alex's favorite, blackberry pie, in the Appendix on pages 196–198.

Your thoughts:

Grand Quotes:

"A little thing is a little thing, but faithfulness in little things is a great thing." (Hudson Taylor)

"I know my grandma loves me because she makes custard for me when I come over." (Clara, age 6)

"Because Peter, our young grandson, enjoyed my baked custard, I felt certain he'd enjoy lime pudding for St. Patrick's Day. He took one bite, shuddered, and said, 'It's too green for me, Grandma.'

"After that, whenever I served my husband green vegetables he didn't like, he'd say, 'It's too green for me, Grandma.'" (Grandma Tea)

31. *Cousins' Day Hosannas*

"Blessed is the king who comes in the name of the Lord!"
"Peace in heaven and glory in the highest!"

Luke 19:38

Read: John 12:12–19

When we plan a Cousins' Day, we invite all five grandkids to get together for a fun time of family bonding with each other. We may attend a children's play, go swimming, cook favorite foods, or draw names and become secret cousins for the day. Sometimes they come for a sleepover. Other times a holiday becomes a great reason to share another Cousins' Day.

One Easter season, we made hot cross buns together then acted out Jesus's triumphal entry, which took place on Palm Sunday. I had pruned ferns to use as palm branches. The grandkids took turns playing Jesus, riding down the sloped yard on the toy motorcycle, while the others waved ferns and shouted, "Hosanna!"

When our oldest grandson, Peter (almost ten), played Jesus, the younger grandkids half-heartedly waved their ferns. Then Clara yelled, "Let's get Peter!" And the chase began to catch "Jesus."

I laughed as I watched their play, but thought, *This isn't what I had planned or what is in the Bible.* And yet . . . maybe it was more realistic than I realized, because in less than a week after Jesus's entry, the crowds no longer honored Him. They, too, were saying, "Let's get Him!"[10]

During holidays or casual gatherings, we can seize the opportunity to intentionally share our faith with our grandkids and also learn from them. I enjoy cooking with our grandchildren, so we create delicious memories and talk about the true meaning of Easter as we cook together. I've included two recipes for you to try. (See Appendix pages 202–204 for Donut Tombs and Empty Tomb Rolls.)

Prayer: Dear Father, thank You for the glorious season of Easter. What a joy to celebrate the triumph of Jesus's resurrection. May we celebrate the joy and power of new life through Christ all year long.

GRAND Thought: Family gatherings and celebrations strengthen family relationships. These events also create teachable moments and provide opportunities to share our faith.

GRAND Response:

1. What ideas do you have for special gatherings with cousins or other family members?

2. Here are ideas from other grandparents:

When Grandma Petey's grandchildren gathered, she planned special projects, such as making stepping-stones for the garden. She also saved her grandchildren's schoolwork, poetry, and stories, and compiled them into a book

10. Devotion adapted from the story in *Preparing My Heart for Grandparenting*, page 150.

for each grandchild, which she printed at the copy center.

Some grandparents host a weeklong or weekend Grand-kid Camp or Cousins' Camp for their grandkids. Building family relationships takes time, energy, and prayer. But it's worth it!

Your thoughts:

Grand Quotes:

"Children enjoy jokes and humor. Our three-year-old grandson loved to say, 'I make a joke' after he said something funny." (Grandma Tea)

"Celebrate silliness. Don't take life too seriously. We're not too sophisticated to have fun." (Great-Grandma Margaret)

"Yes, indeedy, grandkids are the best thing I ever did. Grandkids keep old people alive and laughing." (Grandma Petey)

32. *Celebrate Spiritual Birthdays*

There is rejoicing in the presence of the angels of God over one sinner who repents.

(Luke 15:10)

Read: Luke 15:1-10

Once a year we celebrate all our grandchildren's spiritual birthdays with a special party. When we started this tradition, Clara asked, "Since it's a *birthday* party, will there be gifts?"

"Yes," I assured her. We include all the usual party items—balloons, games, gifts, cake, and ice cream.

All the grandkids are invited, even if they are too young to understand or haven't made a commitment to Jesus yet. Their parents are welcome too.

One year when we planned the party, our grandkids were between the ages of five and eleven. We used a royal theme, and our grandkids wore paper crowns that said "King Jesus" on them. We shared that when we invite Jesus into our hearts, we become children of God. Since Jesus is the King of kings, we are His princes and princesses. That's worth celebrating!

For my royal guests, I prepared their dining chairs with puffy pillows and fringed blankets. Place settings included their framed pictures, and we ate royal foods, such as tortilla crowns and chocolate-dipped pretzel scepters. It was quite a regal event!

I placed a large treasure chest in the backyard with their presents, and the grandkids followed clues to find gifts marked for Prince Peter, Prince Alex, Princess Clara, and Prince Owen. Each of them also received a felt bookmark with the date of their spiritual birthday.

When our grandchildren were older, we used the theme of Jesus is the Rock from Psalm 62:2 ("he is my rock and my salvation"). We gave each grandchild a rock, and they wrote their names and spiritual birthdays on them with felt pens.

Each year's theme is different, but we always celebrate that they have invited Jesus into their hearts, and we pray a blessing over each grandchild's life. Sometimes they write a note to Jesus, telling Him how they want to grow spiritually during the next year. I save their notes in sealed envelopes, and they open them at the next spiritual birthday party. These events are a wonderful time to talk about Jesus and the gift of eternal life.

In the Appendix, pages 179–181, you will find the Path to Salvation, which gives a simple way to share the gospel in ten words. You could teach this to your grandchildren so they can share it with others.

The Appendix also includes royal recipes to prepare for your grandkids or together with them as you talk about Jesus and His gift of eternal life. See page 205 for Golden Tortilla Crowns, pages 213–214 for Royal Rings, and page 215 for Sparkling Scepters.

Prayer: Heavenly Father, thank You for the joy of grand-parenting. Show me fresh ways to celebrate and make memories with my grandchildren. Use me to nurture their spiritual lives while we also have fun together. Draw our hearts closer to each other and to You.

GRAND Thought: Spiritual birthdays are memorable milestones in our grandchildren's lives. God rejoices with us as we celebrate together and pray a blessing over each grandchild's life.

GRAND Response:

1. How can you nurture spiritual growth in your grandchildren? Would you like to plan a spiritual birthday party? If so, record your plans.

2. If your grandchildren are too old for such a party, consider taking them out for dinner and giving them a gift to help them grow spiritually (such as a subscription to a Christian magazine, a devotional book, a Bible, or a plaque with a Bible theme). Gifts are important to grand-kids, but before you buy any, check with their parents on what is appropriate. Then pray about what to give them. It's not how much you spend that matters; it's your heart of love behind it. Give according to your means and as God directs. Don't compare yourself to others. God loves a cheerful giver (2 Corinthians 9:7), so give your gifts with joy from a willing heart.

Your thoughts:

Grand Quotes:

"We can't afford to give a lot of gifts like another set of grandparents does. I prefer to make a memorable experience. I give them a 'proper tea' when they come, and even some of our grandsons look forward to it each time they visit." (Grandma Sylvia)

"When our daughter-in-law, Amy, called to congratulate us on our forty-sixth anniversary, she also shared, 'Anna, became a Christian today.' Hurrah! Another spiritual birthday and a wonderful anniversary gift. We usually celebrate our anniversary by going out to tea. Since then, we include Anna, so we always have a happy Anna-versary!" (Grandpa Milt and Grandma Tea)

33. *I Love You Eighty-Thirty*

May you have the power to understand, as all God's people should, how wide, how long, how high, and how deep his love really is. May you experience the love of Christ, though it is so great you will never fully understand it.

Ephesians 3:18–19 NLT

Read: 1 John 4:9–16

"I'm your valentine," our three-year-old granddaughter Anna announced on Valentine's Day.

"You sure are!" I said giving her a hug when her dad dropped her off for a day with Grandpa and Grandma.

At lunch, Anna wanted her usual tea party with herbal tea and sugar cubes, served in a child-sized teacup. She also enjoyed Grandma's homemade split-pea soup served in a pink, fluted bowl. Since pink is her favorite color, I told her, "This is pink-delicious."

After our tea for three, I leaned over to Anna and said, "I love you."

"I love you too," she replied.

"I love you three," I said with a smile.

"I love you four," she added, figuring out my game.

Grandpa chimed in with, "I love you five," and we were off

and counting, our love growing by the second. Soon it was, "I love you twenty-two," and continued to, "I love you thirty."

Then Anna broke the playful sequence with, "I love you eighty-thirty!" We all laughed, and I hugged Anna.

Anna's big, silly number got me thinking about how that game might go if God and I played it. Maybe I would say, *I love You by the hundreds of thousands.* And God might reply, *I love you billions times trillions,* or *I love you from infinity to infinity.*

But I don't need to play such a game. Although I may not fully understand how wide, how long, or how deep God's love is, He has told me how much He loves me.

"I have loved you with an everlasting love." (Jeremiah 31:3)

"Nothing can ever separate us from God's love. (Romans 8:38 NLT)

"For as high as the heavens are above the earth, so great is his love for those who fear him." (Psalm 103:11)

And that's much more than eighty-thirty!

Prayer: Heavenly Father, thank You for Your everlasting love for my grandchildren and me. Help me model unconditional, Christlike love for my grandchildren. Let them understand more and more how much You love them, and may they respond by following You. In Jesus's name. Amen.

GRAND Thought: God's love is so amazing! It's beyond our understanding. Nothing we can or can't do will make Him love us more or less. God will always love us, because God is love.

GRAND Response:

1. Think of one or two specific ways you can show God's love to your grandchildren. Decide when and how to do so.

2. Before Grandma Elaine leaves after visiting her young grandchildren, she asks, "Are you ready for your secret?" They each come and snuggle up to her while she whispers in their ears: "I love you, and God loves you best of all."

Your thoughts:

Grand Quotes:

"My husband and I had fun with our six-year-old grand-daughter when she came for the afternoon. We packed our bags and pretended to go on vacation. Since our downstairs guest room is always ready for company, it became our hotel room. The three of us relaxed there with books, games, and a cozy blanket. Warm memories remain." (Grandma Tea)

"For us, grandparenting pays in memories, not money. But the memories are more precious than money." (Papa Milt and Grandma Tea)

We Will Serve the Lord

At the graveside of Grandma Tea's parents,
Nicolai and Helena Siemens,
Grandma Tea, Clara Harris, and Peter Faull
thanking God for their godly heritage
("Me and My House," Devotion #39)

Making a GRAND Eternal Impact

(Passing the Baton of Faith from
Generation to Generation)

The devotions in this section relate to the topics in Week Six of *Preparing My Heart for Grandparenting*, pages 172–208.

34. I Came to Have Fun!

The generation of the upright will be blessed.

Psalm 112:2

Read: Psalm 112:1-7

When my husband, Milt, was growing up in Idaho, during the summers he visited his grandparents in Spokane, Washington. Although he didn't regularly attend church, his grandparents took him to Vacation Bible School at their church.

The seeds of faith planted in his childhood bore fruit later. During his college years, Milt invited Jesus into his life. He still has fond memories of his time with Grandpa and Grandma Perkins. When he was in his sixties, we traveled to Spokane to visit the church where he attended VBS.

Milt's grandparents' spiritual investment into his life served as an example to us. During the summers, we invited our grade-school-aged grandsons, Peter and Alex, to stay with us for a week to attend our church's VBS. They enjoyed the mixture of fun games, yummy snacks, and Bible stories.

One memorable summer, our grandsons attended their church's VBS the week before they stayed with us to attend ours.

"Isn't it great that you can learn about Jesus two weeks in a row?" I asked Peter.

He put his hands on his hips and said, "Grandma, I came

to have fun!"

I felt stabbed in the heart. Later I realized this was a typical response for an eight-year-old.

A wise grandma friend said, "Don't worry. He'll learn about Jesus while he has fun."

And he did. At the end of the week, his VBS teacher told me, "Peter prayed to rededicate his life to Jesus this week."

How I rejoiced!

Investing spiritually in our grandchildren's lives is not a small matter. We and our grandchildren reap eternal blessings. Counting back from our grandchildren to Milt's grandparents, their influence has spanned five generations so far. Our grandchildren are their great-great-grandchildren.

Prayer: Dear Father, thank You for those who have sown spiritual seeds into our lives and the lives of our grandchildren. Help us faithfully follow in their footsteps and influence future generations for Jesus.

GRAND Thought: The time we invest in our grandchildren's lives will impact them forever. Generations yet unborn will continue to benefit from the ripple effect of our faith.

GRAND Response:

1. Who has spiritually influenced your life and/or the lives of your grandchildren? Consider writing them a thank-you note or honoring them in some way. If possible, include your grandchildren as you do this. If you are the first generation of believers, how can you start a spiritual ripple effect in your family?

2. Brainstorm ways you can invest spiritually in your grandchildren. What can you do in your home? Consider singing hymns, reading Bible stories, praying together, and establishing spiritual traditions for Christmas and Easter. Then outside your home, what besides VBS is available near you? Could you take your grandchildren to church nativity scenes, Christmas performances, Sunday School, Christian camps, youth groups, or classes offered by the church?

Your thoughts:

Grand Quotes:

"Children, especially the young, can be impacted for a lifetime by the kindness and attention paid by those who tell them about Jesus." (James Dobson, in his VBS letter of July 2007)

"My dad read books to me at night from the time I was very young. He read a children's Bible storybook along with the classics. Grandparents can do that when a grandchild is visiting. I didn't get any doctrine or theology, but I knew all the basic Bible stories, which gave me a love for Jesus and the Bible. With my children, we sang Sunday School songs every night while my husband played the guitar." (Great-Grandma Barbara)

35. *The Green Lizard Bible*

I have no greater joy than to hear that my children [and grandchildren] *are walking in the truth.*

3 John 1:4 (emphasis added)

Read: Psalm 119:9–16

It was my husband's birthday, but someone else was getting a gift. Our six-year-old grandson Owen wanted a Bible—the Adventure green lizard Bible for early readers—and we had purchased it for him.

Although it wasn't a special occasion for Owen, we were thrilled to buy him a Bible. The cost didn't matter to us or that it wasn't Owen's actual birthdate. What mattered was he wanted a Bible now, and we couldn't think of a better investment into his life. It would certainly bring good returns.

Clara, Owen's eight-year-old sister, excited for Owen, asked to present the Bible to her brother. She held it behind her back and said, "We have a surprise for you, Owen." Then she handed him the Bible.

Owen's face was all smiles as he eagerly accepted his gift. He immediately opened the Bible and began reading the few words he knew: "and . . . the . . . God" and books of the Bible, such as John.

Owen sat beside me on the sofa and listened as I read Joshua 1:8 from his New International Reader's Version of the Bible. "Never stop reading this Book of the Law. Day and night you must think about what it says. Make sure you do everything that is written in it. Then things will go well with you. And you will have great success." I read it to myself as much as to Owen. In the front of his Bible, I wrote: "We pray you will always love God's Word."

Grandpa didn't get any wrapped gifts that day. He would receive those at the family party in a few days. But spending time with his grandchildren and seeing Owen's excitement to receive a Bible offered a priceless gift—one with eternal value.

On the day of Grandpa's family celebration, Owen arrived carrying his new Bible. "I want to read from my Bible," he said.

When we were all seated in the living room, Owen randomly opened his Bible to 2 Thessalonians 3:1 (NIRV), and I helped him read aloud Paul's Spirit-inspired words. "Brothers and sisters, pray for us. Pray that the Lord's message will spread quickly. Pray that others will honor it just as you did." Although not planned by Owen, it seemed the perfect verse to read to his grandpa, who has a heart for prayer and loves to pray for his grandchildren and others. And the last sentence, "Pray that others will honor it just as you did," seemed the right words coming from a grandson who loved God's Word.

Prayer: Dear Father, thank You for Your precious Word and the opportunities to share it with others. Thank You for the great joy it brings me when my grandchildren are eager to walk in Your truth. Help me to model an ongoing godly example and a deep love for Your Word.

GRAND Thought: Our greatest joy comes from knowing that our grandchildren and other family members walk in the truth of God's Word.

GRAND Response:

1. How can you grow in your love for God's Word? How can you be more intentional about reading and studying the Bible each day?

2. In what ways can you model this love for your grandchildren? How can you nurture their love for God and His Word? Pray and ask God for fresh ideas, and list them here.

Your thoughts:

Grand Quotes:

"We read the children's Bible together, and they see me reading my Bible. Recently when I had my Bible open, my grandson said, 'You read that every day, don't you?' He sees my living faith—that's important." (Grandma Bonnie)

"My granddaughter (age 21) asked if she could have my Bible after I die." (Grandma Eva)

36. *PLAYing with My Grandkids*

For God so loved the world, that he gave his only begotten Son, that whosoever believeth in him should not perish, but have everlasting life.

John 3:16 KJV

Read: John 14:1-6

My seven-year-old granddaughter Clara and I licked ice cream cones from a favorite ice cream shop as we chatted.

"What's the best book" I asked.

"The Bible," she quickly replied.

"What makes it the best book?" I asked.

"It's about God."

I agreed. "And it tells us how to get to heaven."

Then, on the spur of the moment, we created a little skit, which was a phone conversation between Clara and me.

(Telephone rings.)

Grandma: "Hi, Clara, it's Grandma."

Clara: "Hi, Grandma. Why are you calling?"

Grandma: "I need directions."

Clara: "Where to?"

Grandma: "Heaven. Where do I find directions to heaven?"

Clara: "In the Bible."

Grandma: "Where in the Bible?"

Clara: "John 3:16." (Then she quoted the verse by memory—she had learned it in Awana.)

Grandma: "Thanks, Clara. I'm not ready to go to heaven yet, but now I know how to get there."

Clara: "Okay. You're welcome."

Grandma: "I love you. Bye."

When I brought Clara home, we did the skit for her family. Then I asked her five-year-old brother, Owen, if he'd like to do it with me. He did.

Grandma: "Owen, where can I get directions to heaven?"

Owen: "In the Bible."

Grandma: "Where in the Bible?"

Owen: "Genesis."

Surprised by his answer, I thought for a moment, then said, "Oh, yes, 'In the beginning God created the HEAVENS and the earth.' "

Owen nodded and smiled.

Earlier that evening, while Clara and I talked about the Bible,

I mentioned that Psalm 117 was the shortest chapter in the Bible. Clara immediately turned to it and read aloud: "Praise the Lord, all you nations; extol him, all you peoples." Then she asked, "What does extol mean?"

Before I could think of an answer, she asked, "Does it mean worship?"

Hearing her quick answer to her own question blessed me. We are developing a sweet relationship, and she's helping me grow up as a grandmother.

Now, twelve years later, Clara attends college and has a stack of books to read and study. When I asked her, "What's the best book?" She gave me the same answer: "the Bible."

Prayer: Heavenly Father, thank You for Your precious Word, preserved for us so everyone can come to know You. Your Word is a lamp to our feet, a light to our pathway, and it keeps us from sin (Psalm 119:105, 11).

GRAND Thought: Teaching our grandchildren to love the Bible can be fun. And it brings eternal rewards for them and us.

GRAND Response:

1. How can you help your grandchildren learn to love and obey God's Word?

2. Perhaps you could memorize a verse together with your grandchild, such as John 3:16, John 14:6, 1 John 1:9, or

one of your favorites. Consider letting your grandchild choose which verse to memorize.

3. The song "The B-I-B-L-E" expresses the importance of God's word in our lives. Teach it to a young grandchild, or learn it from the Internet and sing it together. You could also create a short skit together and perform it for your family.

Your thoughts:

Grand Quotes:

"My grandson Braeden (five) was so cute the other day. I had to laugh. He asked me real seriously, 'Do animals bite in heaven? Can you get hurt and die again?' After some discussion and reassuring him that animals would not hurt him in heaven, he said, 'I'm going to ride a cheetah!'" (Great-Grandma Sharon)

"When my granddaughter, Anika came to study the Bible with me, I opened our family Bible to Psalm 119 and placed it on our entry table. In front of it, I placed an index card with verse 103 printed on it. I spooned a dollop of honey onto the verse and invited Anika to taste and see how sweet the Word of God is. She licked the honey from the card, and read aloud, 'How sweet are your words to my taste, sweeter than honey to my mouth.' Her radiant smile told me this was a lesson she would remember and treasure." (Grandma Peggy)

37. *Let's Draw Heaven*

I will dwell in the house of the Lord forever.

Psalm 23:6

Read: Psalm 23

I wanted to connect with my eight-year-old granddaughter, Clara, once or twice a month for spiritual mentoring. One month, the day that worked best for her was on my husband's birthday.

When I picked up Clara, I asked, "Shall we buy Grandpa a card and then kidnap him and take him out for tea or something?" She liked the idea.

I called Grandpa to tip him off. "We plan to kidnap you, so get ready." He was happy to play along.

Driving to our home, we talked about the Bible. Clara said, "I memorized Psalm 23 in Awana."

"Wonderful," I said. "Can you recite it for me?" She did.

I told her that often this psalm is used at memorial services. "Why do you think they choose that psalm?" I asked, having an idea of my own.

"Because it talks about going to heaven. 'I shall dwell in the house of the Lord forever,'" she said.

I had thought of a different verse: "Yea though I walk through the valley of the shadow of death, I will fear no evil" (KJV).

Soon we kidnapped Grandpa and headed to the bakery at a food court. Clara ordered hot chocolate with whipped cream and a snickerdoodle cookie. Grandpa and I shared a pot of spiced tea and a pumpkin muffin.

After our treats, Grandpa listened in as Clara and I talked about Psalm 23. We drew simple pictures in our journals about the six verses, including sheep, a shepherd, a quiet river, and green grass. We also talked about why we need Jesus as our Shepherd to lead us and how we would behave if we were following Him in *paths of righteousness*.

Clara immediately said, "I wouldn't argue with my brother."

For the last verse, about dwelling in the house of the Lord forever, Clara suggested, "Let's draw a picture of heaven."

"I don't know what heaven looks like," I said.

Clara didn't hesitate. She drew Jesus, their family's golden retriever that had died, and people she loved who were already with Jesus—a great-grandmother and her mom's close friend.

My page remained blank as I considered how to draw streets of gold.

Clara had the right idea. She wasn't concerned about how heaven looked, only about who was waiting for her there.

And I wondered, *Who's teaching whom?*

Prayer: Dear Father, thank You for the blessing of grand-children and their spiritual insights. You want us to come to You like a little child. Give me childlike faith and a teachable spirit. May I learn from my grandchildren and from Your Word. Also, help me to be prepared to give an answer to others for the hope that I have in You (1 Peter 3:15).

GRAND Thought: Spending time in God's Word and exploring spiritual truths with our grandchildren will boost their faith and ours. We can learn from each other.

GRAND Response:

1. How do you picture heaven? How would you explain heaven to your grandchildren?

2. How can you grow in your Bible knowledge so you have answers for your grandchildren and others? Could you learn through personal Bible reading or group Bible studies (for example: church Bible studies, online studies, and community groups such as Bible Study Fellowship)?

Your thoughts:

Grand Quotes:

"We can offer a biblical perspective to our grandchildren as we share about life and death." (Grandma Tea)

My daughter-in-law was discussing with her young daughter how God took care of the Israelites when they wandered in the wilderness. "Do you remember what God fed them each day?"

"Manna-cotti," Clara replied. (Grandma Tea)

"After I told my young grandson about the Israelites traveling to a land flowing with milk and honey, he had an idea. We headed to the kitchen, and he asked me to help him mix milk and honey. Then he took a sip of his creation and proclaimed, 'Delicious!'" (A grandmother)

38. *Tell Me a Story*

We will tell the next generation the praiseworthy deeds of the LORD, his power, and the wonders he has done.

Psalm 78:4

Read: Psalm 145:4-13

When I told my teenage grandson I was turning seventy, he asked, "What have you been doing all those years?"

I laughed. "Well, for one thing, I raised two children, and one is your mother."

He smiled and nodded.

"After that? Time with five grandchildren!"

Although I chuckled at Peter's question, it prompted me to think about my past seventy years and to thank God for His blessings and help during challenging seasons. It also encouraged me to jot down highlights of each decade, so I could intentionally share snippets of my life with my grandkids.

Over lunch on our wedding anniversary, I had two stories ready to share with them from our courting days. "Would you like to hear the 'Torn Pants' story or the 'Old Shoes' story? I prompted. Of course, they wanted to hear both. The stories were simple and somewhat funny, and they got to know more about Grandpa Milt during his college days when we were dating.

Grandparents Day in September is a great time to share faith-building stories and life events with your grandchildren. What "praiseworthy deeds of the Lord" can you tell?

Here are a few questions to help you recall how God has worked in your life. Each one triggers stories for me.

How did God answer a specific prayer?

How did God provide a job during difficult times?

How did God comfort you during a loss?

Is there a special verse God used to build your faith or to help you through a hard time?

How did someone encourage you or pray for you when you needed courage?

Your answers to these questions and others are all part of your life story and will bless your children and grandchildren.

Whenever my parents came to visit while we raised our family, our children begged, "Tell us a story." Grandpa was always ready and eager to comply. Through his personal stories and Bible stories, they learned valuable lessons from Grandpa's life and his faith in Christ, which still impact them today.

Prayer: Heavenly Father, thank You for the blessing of children and grandchildren. Help me see Your fingerprints in my life so I can share Your power, wonders, and praise-worthy deeds with my grandchildren and others.

GRAND Thought: Sharing our life's milestones glorifies God and creates a lasting legacy of meaningful memories for our grandchildren and us.

GRAND Response:

1. When you get together with your grandchildren, share faith-building stories from your life with them. You could take them out for a treat, invite them over for a root beer float, share a simple snack, or enjoy a picnic.

2. If your grandchildren don't live nearby, you could call them, have an online video meeting, or relate your memories and faith stories in writing or on a recorded video. Which of these ideas would work for you? Jot down several specific stories so you will be ready to share them when your grandchildren say, "Tell me a story."

3. Our son and daughter-in-law created a shadow box with small mementos inside to remind them of God's provision and protection. For example, a small wooden heart with a hole in it reminds them of their son's successful open-heart surgery as a toddler. The shadow box hangs on their kitchen wall, so they can tell their children and others what God has done.

Your thoughts:

Grand Quotes:

When I told my granddaughter, Anna, I was seventy, she said, "You don't seem that old."

"How old do I seem?" I asked.

"About the age of my friends."

Wow, that made me only six years old! And it was a great compliment that she could relate to me as a friend. (Grandma Tea)

"We don't wait to talk about Jesus until we are praying or having a Bible lesson. We relate our spiritual values to everyday situations and watch for opportunities to bring the reality of Jesus into our grandkids' lives." (Grandma Shirley)

39. *Me and My House*

As for me and my house, we will serve the LORD.

Joshua 24:15 KJV

Read: Joshua 24:14–18

One Memorial Day weekend, Peter and Clara, our nine- and five-year-old grandchildren, came for a fun afternoon with Grandpa and me. Before we took them to the beach, I decided to stop at the cemetery and visit my parents' gravesite.

I read the words engraved on my parents' stone aloud: "As for me and my house, we will serve the LORD." I explained that after my father died, I had asked Mother which verse she wanted on their tombstone. She chose Joshua 24:15 and said, "Me and my house includes everybody."

"Your great-grandma was thinking of *you* when she chose that verse," I said. "She wanted everyone in her family to love Jesus and follow Him." We sat on the ground by the gravesite, bowed our heads, and thanked God for our godly heritage. (See photo, page 146.) My parents weren't rich materially, but they passed on priceless spiritual treasures to future generations. We can too.

Remembering the verse my mother chose for their gravestone, I realize her desire went beyond words carved on stone. She wanted her faith engraved on the hearts of her descendants. God honored her longing and godly example.

My mother's eight children wholeheartedly embraced her faith in Jesus. The ripple effect of godliness continues to the next generations of twelve grandchildren and twenty-three great-grandchildren (most born after she died). To God be the glory!

As intentional Christian grandparents, my husband and I yearn to pass on a godly legacy. No doubt you do too. With God's help, we can pass the baton of faith into the hands of future generations and say, "As for me and my house, we will serve the Lord!"

Prayer: Heavenly Father, thank You for the priceless inheritance You're keeping for us in heaven. It's one that won't perish, spoil, or fade. I want to lay up a rich heritage for my grandchildren and those I love. May they see that my faith in Jesus is real and desire it for themselves. By Your Spirit, draw each grandchild and others I love to You. Just as You are faithful, Lord, help *me* to be faithful, unwavering, always abounding in Your work, knowing that my labor is not in vain. Help me to fight the good fight and to keep the faith so future generations yet unborn will learn about Your power and faithfulness and love and follow You all their days (based on 1 Peter 1:4; 1 Corinthians 15:58; 2 Timothy 4:7; Psalm 78:4–7).[11]

GRAND Thought: No matter how rich or poor we are, we can give our grandchildren a tremendous gift—a legacy of

11. Devotion adapted from *Preparing My Heart for Grandparenting*, pages 172 and 179.

faith. We will influence not only the present generation but all future generations, even after we're gone. Never underestimate the power of a grandparent's faith in God!

GRAND Response:

1. What legacy do you want to leave your grandchildren and others you are influencing?

2. What plans can you make to begin, continue, or strengthen what you're already doing? Ask God for His wisdom and guidance to do so.

3. You'll find an inspirational poem about grandparenting, "Tending the Family Tree" by Greg Asimakoupoulos, on page 191 in the Appendix.

Your thoughts:

Grand Quotes:

"I remember Bible stories, biblical principles, and lessons Grandpa taught me as a child, and I've saved a journal of stories he wrote for me. His wisdom helped shape my Christian worldview and still impacts how I live my life and teach my children." (Granddaughter, Joan)

"The most beautiful sight at our home is my husband daily on his knees. With his Bible open, Milt prays for our family from the Scripture verses he has just read. Then on Sundays, he often emails our adult children and me the verse he prayed for us. What a blessing!" (Grandma Tea)

40. *Passing the Baton*

*Future generations will be told about the Lord.
They will proclaim his righteousness to a people yet unborn.*

Psalm 22:30–31

Read: Psalm 22:25–31

Our four-day family reunion was coming to a close. Three generations, ranging in age from one month to seventy-two years, had gathered to reconnect and share God's faithfulness.

We recalled many important memories, such as how our father was miraculously released from a Russian prison during the same hour his brother's church in America prayed for his deliverance. As we shared our lives, we saw strong evidence of God's love and blessings all around us, including the twelve preschool-age children born into our families. Two of these were our grandsons.

We also sang songs about God's faithfulness and goodness. "To Every Generation" is one of the songs that holds meaning for us. The words are adapted from Psalm 90:1 (NKJV), which is a prayer of Moses. "Lord, You have been our dwelling place in all generations." (You can find the words and music online.)

Our son, Jonathan, wrote and added his own verse and melody to this song. He took the words from Psalm 78:4–7:

"We will proclaim Your deeds to our children;
The mighty deeds of the Lord.
And even those who are yet unborn
Will learn about Your power
And of Your faithfulness
And love and follow You all their days."

The powerful verses in Psalm 78 encourage us to think about the impact we can make, not only on our children, but also on all the generations yet to be born.

As we concluded our reunion, I found myself thinking of that future reunion in heaven and prayed that no one in our family would be missing. We formed a large circle and passed a "baton of faith" from hand to hand. As we did so, each person said, "I will be faithful to Jesus and follow in His footsteps." Slowly, the baton traveled around the group. It came full circle when my niece's son passed it to me with tears in his eyes, repeating what each member had said, "I will be faithful to Jesus and follow in His footsteps."

As a Christian family, it is our deep desire to tell future generations about the Lord and to proclaim God's righteousness to generations not yet born. Family reunions are one way we can intentionally share our faith and reconnect with loved ones.

Prayer: Precious heavenly Father, You are the gracious Ruler over all the families of the earth. With grateful hearts, we remember Your goodness to our family. You have blessed us and been our Shelter for many generations. As we run our race on earth, help us to finish strong and to pass the baton of faith securely into the hands of those following us. We trust You with our lives and the lives of our children and grandchildren. May our families and all future generations worship You alone. In Jesus's mighty name. Amen.[12]

GRAND Thought: As we live godly lives, the generational blessings we leave behind for our present and future grandchildren are beyond anything we can imagine.

GRAND Response:

1. In what ways can you pass on your faith to your family? Ask God for ideas to share your faith and blessings with future generations.

2. Consider praying a blessing over each of your grandchildren. You could conclude your prayer with the blessing found in Numbers 6:24–26.

The LORD bless you and keep you (add grandchild's name)*; the LORD make his face shine upon you and be gracious to you; the LORD turn his face toward you and give you peace.*

I pray in the name of the Father, Son, and Holy Spirit. Amen.

3. You can find recordings of "The Blessing," a song with the words from Numbers 6:24–26, on the internet. You could listen to it with your grandchildren or sing it to them.

---

12. Devotion adapted from *Preparing My Heart for Grandparenting*, pages 207–208.

You can learn more about the biblical concept of passing on a blessing in *The Blessing,* written by Gary Smalley and John Trent.

Your thoughts:

Grand Quotes:

"I can be one of my grandchildren's best memories. Although I may die in their lifetime, I want to leave them with a positive picture of God." (Grandma Debbie)

"Some years ago, while I battled cancer, my son, Jonathan, blessed me with a special birthday gift. He made a recording of 'To Every Generation' that included the words and melody he wrote. He played the guitar, French horn, sang, and then mixed them all together in one recording. It soothed my heart to see another generation continue the faith and heritage passed on to me by my godly parents." (Grandma Tea)

Conclusion:

As you finish this devotional book, may it be only the beginning of God working in greater ways in your life and the lives of your grandchildren. To conclude, I pray these verses from Psalm 115:14–15 (with emphasis added) over you:

"May the LORD cause you to flourish,
both you and your children [and grandchildren].
May you be blessed by the LORD,
the Maker of heaven and earth."

Together with you in love, prayer, and grandparenting,

Grandma Tea

APPENDIX

PART ONE

Sharing Your Faith with Your Grandchildren

Path to Salvation

These verses will help you begin a new relationship with God. They explain how to invite Him to become the loving leader in your life.

1. God loves.

"For God so loved the world that he gave his one and only Son, that whoever believes in him shall not perish but have eternal life." (John 3:16)

God loves you and created you for a purpose. He wants to have a personal relationship with you.

2. We sinned.

"For all have sinned and fall short of the glory of God." (Romans 3:23)

Because of our sins (disobeying God and going our own way), we are separated from a holy (sinless) God.

3. Jesus died.

"But God demonstrates his own love for us in this: While we were still sinners, Christ died for us." (Romans 5:8)

God made a plan to bring us into a relationship with Him. He sent His Son to die to save us from our sins.

4. God forgives.

"If we confess our sins, he is faithful and just and will forgive us our sins and purify us from all unrighteousness." (1 John 1:9)

If we turn from our sins and ask for forgiveness, God will forgive us.

5. We accept.

"Yet to all who received him, to those who believed in his name, he gave the right to become children of God." (John 1:12)

Once we accept God's gift of salvation, which comes only through Jesus, we become part of God's family. If you want to turn your life over to God, pray a prayer something like this:

Dear God, I know I'm a sinner. Thank You for sending Jesus to die for me. Please forgive my sins. I want to turn from my wrongdoings and receive Jesus as my Savior. Thank You for forgiving me. I give You control of my life and want to follow You. In Jesus's name. Amen.

If you prayed this prayer as an act of faith, then 2 Corinthians 5:17 is true of you:

"Anyone who believes in Christ is a new creation. The old is gone! The new has come!" (NIRV)

To grow in Christ:

1. Tell others of your new faith in Christ.

2. Find and attend a church that solidly teaches the Word of God.

3. Talk to God in prayer every day, and read the Bible—His love letter to you.

You can receive a free daily devotional at https://billygraham.org/devotions. If you have questions or need help to grow in your faith, e-mail: help@bgea.org or call 1-877-247-2426.

(Excerpted from *Preparing My Heart for Grandparenting*, pages 209–210.)

PART TWO

Prayer Tips and Teaching

How to Pray for Your Grandchildren

(Devotion 7)

When and where to pray:

1. Pray for your grandchildren before they are conceived. Ask God to make you into the grandparent they need.

2. After conception and during the pregnancy, begin praying for your grandbaby's development—physically, spiritually, mentally, and emotionally. Pray for wisdom and special sensitivity toward each grandchild.

3. Pray in their rooms. God's presence can fill a place so that it affects what happens there. When you visit, step into their rooms and pray. God will guide you in your prayers.

4. Make prayer a way of life, more than just during devotions. Pray with them when they have a concern. Thank God with them when they are happy. Pray with them for forgiveness when they do something wrong. Pray with them at different times and places so they know they can talk to God anytime, anywhere.

5. Look for opportunities for special prayer times. While you're away from your grandchildren, ask God for ideas of what to do when you are with them again. You can also pray with them over the phone or send written prayers.

Why to pray:

1. Realize your grandchildren have spiritual potential. They can learn spiritual truths and become Christians at a young age. God listens just as closely to their prayers as He does to yours.

2. Believe in their spiritual potential. Grandparents can make a big difference as they recognize and affirm their grandchildren's gifts and help develop them.

What to pray:

1. Your prayers will make a difference in your newborn grandbaby's life. Ask God to bless and protect the infant, to give him/her a sense of security and of being loved by you and God, and for a responsive heart toward God.

2. You will teach your grandchildren truths about God as you pray with them.

3. Teach them to pray for others' needs, praying until the answer comes. Give thanks with them when God answers.

4. Share your needs with them. It will form bonds between you as they pray for you and realize you value their prayers.

5. Pray for the healing of their spirits. Ask God to help you be sensitive to their hurts and to see those hurts from their perspective. Pray for God to touch and heal their emotions so hurts don't build up.

6. If your grandchildren are adopted or are foster children, pray for every part of their lives before they

joined your family. If possible, pray for them by their bedsides while they sleep.

7. If there is a problem or you are having difficulty with your grandchild, begin by asking God to change you first. Ask God, "Is there anything in me that needs to be different so you can work more effectively in this situation?"

8. Any time we pray we become a prayer partner with Jesus for them. Ask God to bring your children and grandchildren to your mind whenever they need help. Then as you think of them, respond with a moment of prayer. The more you do this, the more you will sense their needs and how to pray for them.

How to Pray with Your Grandchildren

1. Pray in their world by praying simple age-appropriate prayers and for things important to them. In 1 Corinthians 13:11 it says, "When I was a child . . . I thought like a child." Don't make them pray in your world. Instead, pray about things that are important to them, rather than teaching them a memorized prayer that might not cover their needs. For example, if young children learn that God will help them learn to skip, then as teens they can believe God will help them deal with loneliness and later with financial pressures and marriage. Positive experiences as young children strengthen their faith for more crucial things later.

2. Pray with them rather than at them. If you use prayer as a means of disciplining them (telling God all the things they have done wrong), they won't want to pray. Your grandchildren may learn more from your example in prayer than from what you pray for them.

3. Focus on the positive and be joyful with them. Take a few steps back and look at your own conversation. How much of it is corrective? Make your times with your grandchildren special and affirm them. God has special plans for them. Make your prayers positive rather than corrective.

(Adapted from a Prayerlife audiotape, "Your Personal Prayer Life," by Glaphre Gilliland.)

Four-Step Prayer Format
(from Moms in Prayer)
(Devotion 9)

Step One: Praise God

Praising God means focusing on Him and who He is. When we praise Him, we're not praying for others or ourselves; we're thinking about God and His attributes. Is He loving? Is He trustworthy? Yes, of course. That's what we tell Him as we praise Him for *who* He is not for what He does in answer to our prayers.

Using a Scripture passage or a worship song helps me focus on God's specific attributes and give Him praise. The Bible is full of passages that express praise to God.

Although I joined a Moms in Touch group to make requests for my children, now my favorite part of our grandmothers' prayer time is praising God. "I will call upon the LORD, who is worthy to be praised" (Psalm 18:3 KJV).

Step Two: Confess Sins

We ask God to search our hearts and confess any sins He reveals, asking for His forgiveness. It's a time to let God scrub us clean. In a prayer group, confession is usually done silently.

Psalm 66:18 gives us a good reason to repent. *"If I had*

cherished sin in my heart, the Lord would not have listened." As 1 John 1:9 reminds us, when we confess, God forgives.

Step Three: Thank God
We thank God for answered prayers.

"Enter his gates with thanksgiving and his courts with praise; give thanks to him and praise his name. For the LORD is good." (Psalm 100:4–5)

God loves to hear us thank Him. The story in Luke 17:11–19 tells about Jesus healing ten lepers. Sadly, only one returned to thank Him. Can't you hear the disappointment in Jesus's voice when He asked, "Were not all ten cleansed? Where are the other nine?" (v. 17).

I don't want to be like the nine lepers who didn't return to say thanks. But sometimes I forget to thank God for answers to prayer. One way to remember God's faithfulness is to record your prayers and God's answers in a journal.

Psalm 50:23 says, *"He who offers a sacrifice of praise and thanksgiving honors Me"* (AMP).

Step Four: Intercede for Grandchildren
We bring our concerns and requests to God.

God is concerned about whatever concerns you, His child. Nothing is too big or too small to pray about. *"You can throw the whole weight of your anxieties upon him, for you are his personal concern"* (1 Peter 5:7 PHILLIPS).

Talk to God about your concerns, and pray for His will in your grandchildren's lives. Then watch God work!

Praise + confession + thanksgiving + intercession = prayer power!

Adapted from *Preparing My Heart for Grandparenting*, pages 36–42.

PART THREE

Poems

Litany of Love

A Celebration of Peter's Second Birthday!

(Devotion 2)

Before the foundation of the earth, God planned for Peter's birth.
We love you, Peter, and we're glad you were born!

God formed Peter's inmost parts and knit him together in his mother's womb.
We love you, Peter, and we're glad you were born!

God answered our prayers so Peter was born healthy and right on time.
We love you, Peter, and we're glad you were born!

Peter is fearfully and wonderfully made.
We love you, Peter, and we're glad you were born!

The day of Peter's birthday was an exciting day. Grandma and Grandpa Faull, Grandma and Grandpa Harris, Jon and Amy, David, and Bailey visited him in the hospital.
We love you, Peter, and we're glad you were born!

God created Peter with a cheerful personality, a joyful laugh, and a ready smile.
We love you, Peter, and we're glad you were born!

God made Peter with a tender, loving heart, and he likes to give hugs.
We love you, Peter, and we're glad you were born!

Peter enlivens our lives as we watch him dance and enjoy music.
We love you, Peter, and we're glad you were born!

Peter showed an interest in prayer from an early age and likes to pray to Jesus.
We love you, Peter, and we're glad you were born!

Peter delights the hearts of his parents, grandparents, and others.
We love you, Peter, and we're glad you were born!

God has a special purpose for Peter's life.
We love you, Peter, and we're glad you were born!

Today we celebrate God's goodness to us in the gift of Peter.
We love you, Peter, and we're glad you were born!

Today we celebrate that Peter is two. Happy birthday, dear Peter!
We love you, Peter, and we're glad you were born!

A Birthday Ode for Owen

Based on Psalm 139
(Devotion 29)

God saw baby Owen before he was born.
Owen, you're two, and we love you!
God created each inch of his unique little form.
Owen, you're two, and we love you!

God planned each day before Owen could breathe.
Owen, you're two, and we love you!
God knew when he'd crawl, and knew when he'd teethe.
Owen, you're two, and we love you!

God thinks about Owen all the time, constantly.
Owen, you're two, and we love you!
God's thoughts far outnumber the sands by the sea.
Owen, you're two, and we love you!

God knows every thought Owen thinks in his head.
Owen, you're two, and we love you!
God knows when he wakes or sleeps in his bed.
Owen, you're two, and we love you!

God sees Owen's heart as he tenderly prays.
Owen, you're two, and we love you!
God watches over him closely through dark nights and days.
Owen, you're two, and we love you!

God had a great purpose for creating our Owen.
Owen, you're two, and we love you!
God fulfills His plan, and Owen keeps growin'.
Owen, you're two, and we love you!

God has kept Owen safe during two precious years.
Owen, you're two, and we love you!
Sometimes there was laughter. Sometimes there were tears.
Owen, you're two, and we love you!

God will take care of Owen for the rest of his life.
Owen, you're two, and we love you!
God will bless him with friends and maybe a wife.
Owen, you're two, and we love you!

We're thankful for Owen in our family tree.
Owen, you're two, and we love you!
He's a treasured addition. Yes, we all will agree!
Owen, you're two, and we love you!

We celebrate your birthday. We thank God for YOU!
Owen, you're two, and we love you!
May God bless and keep you during this year so NEW.
Owen, you're two, and God loves you!

Hooray! Blessed Birthday! How we love God and YOU.

When Owen turned seventeen, we celebrated at a favorite restaurant and gave him another copy of this poem.

Tending the Family Tree
(A grandparent's charge)
by Greg Asimakoupoulos

A tender shoot sprouts from a tree
That's rooted in a trunk called me.
That little branch born from my seed
will grow into a limb.

And how it grows depends on much.
Their parents' guidance, friends, and such.
But, Lord, I know Your grand design
includes grandparents too.

How straight and strong that branch will grow
will be determined (I well know)
by words of blessing, loving touch,
and what grandkids observe.

Lord, may my children's children see
Your Holy Spirit's work in me
through what I do and what I say
and how I make them feel.

A final charge and biblical mandate
from God's Word:

*Only be careful, and watch yourselves closely so that you
do not forget the things your eyes have seen or let them
fade from your heart as long as you live. Teach them to
your children and to their children after them.*

Deuteronomy 4:9

PART FOUR
Recipe Index

1. Anna's Favorite Caramel Strawberries

Fun to eat for a tasty treat.

Gather
fresh whole strawberries
sour cream
brown sugar

Make

1. Wash the strawberries and remove the stems.

2. Spoon sour cream and brown sugar into separate small bowls. Serve with fresh, whole strawberries.

3. Each person helps themselves to the berries, brown sugar, and sour cream.

4. Dip each strawberry into the sour cream and then into the brown sugar. Take a bite, and enjoy the sweet, juicy burst of flavor. You'll want more than one strawberry.

5. Serve four to six berries per person.

Variation: Other fruits, such as grapes, apples, and bananas, also taste delicious dipped in sour cream and brown sugar.

Anna likes to dip her strawberries again and again (we call it double dipping), so I prepare individual small bowls of sour cream and brown sugar for each of us.

Adapted from *In the Kitchen with Grandma: Stirring Up Tasty Memories Together*, page 118.

2. Apple Strudel

A delicious dessert.

Gather

1 (16 oz.) box phyllo dough pastry sheets, thawed
1 (21 oz.) can apple pie filling
1/4 cup butter, melted (salted or unsalted)
3 T. granulated sugar

Make

1. Preheat the oven to 375°. Line a cookie sheet with parchment paper.

2. For each strudel, you need six sheets of phyllo dough. Place two sheets of phyllo dough on a large piece of waxed paper. Brush the dough lightly with melted butter; sprinkle with one tablespoon of sugar.

3. Repeat two more times, adding two sheets of dough, butter, and sugar each time. Stack the six sheets of dough on top of each other.

4. Place the phyllo dough lengthwise on the baking sheet. Spread about one cup filling along one long edge, but leave one inch on the two shorter sides without filling.

5. Fold in each side of the phyllo dough that has no filling. Then roll up the dough and filling, ending with the seam side down. Brush the top with melted butter and sprinkle with sugar.

6. Repeat these steps for each strudel. If you make several, you'll need more butter and sugar. (Strudel can be baked or frozen unbaked to use later.)

7. To bake, place the seam side down on the baking sheet. Cut three or four slits on top of the strudel to vent.

8. Bake for 15 to 20 minutes, until golden brown. If frozen, defrost 30 minutes before baking; bake slightly longer.

9. Serve warm with ice cream or whipped cream. Makes about 3 or 4 servings per strudel. But it's so delicious, you may wish you could eat an entire strudel.

Variations:

1. Use blueberry, peach, or cherry pie filling.

2. To make your own apple filling: peel and coarsely chop baking apples, such as Granny Smith. Microwave the apples until cooked but not mushy. Add cinnamon and nutmeg to taste. Combine sugar or sweetener and 1 tablespoon cornstarch. (Use about 1/2 cup sugar for three cups of apples.) Combine the sugar mixture with apples and return to the microwave for one or two minutes or until thickened.

APPLE STRUDEL

3. Blackberry Pie

Alex's Favorite.

Gather

For Fruit Filling

    4 cups blackberries (thaw if frozen)

    1 to 1 1/4 cups sugar (to taste)

    3 T. tapioca

    1 T. flour

    1 T. butter

Pastry for Crust

    2 cups flour

    1 tsp. salt

    2/3 cup shortening

    1/4 cup cold water (add more if needed)

    1 tsp. coarse or granulated sugar to sprinkle on top, optional

Make

1. Preheat oven to 425°.

2. For filling, combine sugar, tapioca, and flour in a large bowl. Mix in berries. Set aside.

3. For crust, mix flour and salt in another large bowl. Cut in shortening until particles are the size of peas.

4. Add water a tablespoon at a time to moisten flour mixture. Mix with a fork. Gather dough into a ball and divide in half for a two-crust pie.

5. Roll out one-half of the dough on pastry cloth or floured surface. Roll until 1/8-inch thick and a 10-inch circle, about one inch larger than a 9-inch pie pan.

6. Place bottom crust in pan. Add fruit mixture. Dot with small pieces of butter.

7. Roll out second crust the same way and place on top of fruit.

8. Cut off extra dough around the edge of the pie pan. Seal edges and form a fluted edge.

9. Cut a few slits in the top crust. Sprinkle with sugar if desired.

10. Place pie on cookie sheet to catch any juice that may run over while baking.

11. Bake for 15 minutes. Reduce heat to 375° and bake 30 to 45 minutes more until crust is golden brown and the filling bubbles. Place on cooling rack to cool for several hours to thicken.

12. Serve with ice cream or whipped cream, if desired.

Variations: Substitute marionberries, boysenberries, loganberries, blueberries, or mixed berries for blackberries.

Adapted from *In the Kitchen with Grandma: Stirring Up Tasty Memories Together*, pages 156–157.

BLACKBERRY PIE

4. Chocolate Pudding Cones

Plant a candy seed and watch it sprout into a
marshmallow flower.

Gather

1 package (3.9 oz) instant chocolate pudding
1 cup milk
2 cups frozen whipped topping, thawed
12 chocolate sandwich cookies
12 rainbow ice cream cones, flat bottoms (rainbow
    cones come in a package with red, green, and brown
    cones; regular flat cones are also fine)
12 large marshmallows
colored sugar sprinkles
small candy for flower center and "seed," such as
    M&M'S® or small gumdrops
clean kitchen scissors

Make

1. In a large bowl and using a wire whip, beat together
   pudding mix and milk for about two minutes.

2. Blend in whipped topping.

3. Place cookies in a large resealable plastic bag and
   crush them with a rolling pin.

4. Mix half the cookie crumbs into the pudding. Save the
   rest for later.

5. Refrigerate the pudding until ready to serve.

6. To serve, place two teaspoons of crushed cookies into
   the bottom of each cone. Add a candy "seed."

7. Spoon pudding into cones and fill until level with the

top. Sprinkle crushed cookie crumbs on top to resemble dirt. Push down with the back of a spoon.

8. Top with marshmallow flowers. (See directions below.)

9. Eat your chocolate pudding cone as you would an ice cream cone, before it gets soggy. (You could also eat the pudding out of the cone with a teaspoon.)

Makes about 2 1/2 cups pudding for 10 to 12 pudding cones.

Rocky Road Variation: Add 1/2 cup miniature marshmallows and 1/3 cup chopped walnuts to the pudding.

To make marshmallow flowers:

1. Place the rounded side of a marshmallow in your hand (like a log). Flatten it slightly between the palms of your hands.

2. Cut each marshmallow into five pieces using kitchen scissors.

3. Dip cut sides into colored sugar. If fingers get too sticky, dip fingers into cornstarch.

4. Arrange five petals on top of each pudding cone; add a small candy center. Add a fresh mint leaf if desired.

5. These marshmallow flowers also look cute on cupcakes and brighten up other desserts too.

Perky posy variation: Instead of decorating with marshmallow flowers, decorate with a fresh, plastic, or silk flower. Stick a two-inch piece of green straw into the pudding, and place a colorful flower into the straw, stem first.

CHOCOLATE PUDDING CONES

5. Donut Tombs

Quick and easy for young children.

Gather
1 donut
2 donut holes

Make

1. Stand half a donut on a small plate with a donut hole "tombstone" in front.

2. Roll away (eat) the "stone," and reveal the empty tomb!

Ready for Easter

Clara Harris, Alex Faull, Owen and Anna Harris,
Peter Faull

6. Empty Tomb Rolls

The marshmallows inside melt,
leaving a sweet-tasting center.

Delicious for breakfast or dessert.

Gather

1 tube refrigerated crescent rolls or biscuits
8 large marshmallows
2 T. butter, melted
2 T. sugar
2 tsp. cinnamon

Make

1. Preheat the oven to 375°. Line a baking sheet with foil or parchment paper.

2. Separate rolls into triangles, or flatten each biscuit.

3. In a small bowl, mix the sugar and cinnamon.

4. Dip marshmallows into melted butter, then coat with cinnamon-sugar mixture.

5. Place one coated marshmallow on each roll or biscuit and wrap it in dough. Pinch seams together to seal them so marshmallows don't ooze out while baking.

6. Place rolls seam down on the baking sheet. Brush with remaining butter and sprinkle with cinnamon-sugar.

7. Bake 8 to 10 minutes or until golden brown.

8. Cool slightly before eating. (Melted marshmallow in the center will be hot.)

Just like the tomb on Easter Sunday, these rolls are empty!

Makes 8 rolls, but this recipe can be doubled. (They're so yummy, you'll want seconds.)

These rolls are perfect for teaching grandkids the Easter story. Each ingredient has symbolism:

- Marshmallow—Jesus's body
- Butter, cinnamon, and sugar—oil and spices used to anoint Jesus's body
- Dough—burial clothes that Jesus was wrapped in
- Roll—the tomb
- Hole inside the roll after it's baked—the empty tomb following the resurrection of Jesus

7. Golden Tortilla Crowns

Just right for regal princes and princesses.

My grandson, Owen, and I created this recipe together.

Gather
2 6-inch flour tortillas
1/2 cup finely grated cheddar cheese
sliced green or black olives for jewels
carrot circles or diced red and green peppers for jewels

Make
1. Cut tortillas in half with a pizza cutter.
2. The straight edge is the bottom of your crown. Starting in the middle of the rounded edge, cut out two V-shaped notches—one on each side—to make the points of a crown. Repeat for each tortilla half.
3. Place crowns on a microwave-safe plate. Top each crown with grated cheese.
4. Add olive or vegetable jewels.
5. Microwave for 30 seconds, or until the cheese melts.
6. Tortillas will be soft and hot. Handle carefully.
7. Eat them with your best regal manners.

Variation: For crisp cinnamon-and-sugar crowns, spray tortillas with cooking spray, place on a cookie sheet, and sprinkle with cinnamon and sugar. Bake at 350° for 5 minutes or until crisp.

Recipe from *In the Kitchen with Grandma: Stirring Up Tasty Memories Together,* page 150.

8. Grandma's Blueberry Tarts

You can substitute wild "huckles" if available.

Gather (Crust for Tart Shells)
    1 cup all-purpose flour
    1 tsp. sugar
    1/4 tsp. salt
    1/3 cup shortening or butter
    2 to 3 T. cold water

Make

1. Preheat the oven to 450°. Spray muffin cups with non-stick cooking spray.

2. Combine the dry ingredients.

3. Cut in the shortening or butter.

4. Add water to moisten.

5. Mix well, and roll 1/8-inch thick on a floured surface.

6. With a 3-inch cookie cutter, cut 12 circles from the dough.

7. Place circles in muffin tins to make tart shells. Prick sides and bottoms 3 or 4 times to prevent puffing.

8. Bake for 5 to 9 minutes until lightly browned. Cool in muffin tin.

Makes 12.

Gather (Fresh Blueberry Filling)
    1 1/3 cups fresh blueberries, divided
    1/2 cup granulated sugar
    1 T. cornstarch

1 T. water
1 tsp. lemon juice
whipped cream for topping
fresh mint leaves for garnish, optional

Make

1. In a 1-quart saucepan, combine sugar and cornstarch.

2. Stir in water and lemon juice.

3. Add and mash in 1/3 cup berries.

4. Bring to a boil; simmer a few minutes to thicken, stirring frequently. Remove from heat.

5. When sauce is cool, gently stir in one cup fresh berries. Refrigerate until ready to serve.

6. Spoon berry filling into tart shells. Top with whipped cream. Garnish each tart with a sprig of mint and a few berries.

Owen Harris with the
Huckleberry Tarts he made (Devotion 24)

9. Homemade Maple-Flavored Syrup
Easy and inexpensive to make.

Gather

1 cup granulated sugar
1 cup packed brown sugar
1 cup water
1/2 tsp. maple flavoring
salt (optional)

Make

1. Pour both sugars and water into a saucepan.

2. Cook over medium heat until sugar dissolves and syrup comes to a boil, stirring frequently with a wooden spoon. Boil syrup for one minute.

3. Remove from heat. Stir in maple flavoring and a dash of salt.

Makes 1 1/2 cups syrup.

Refrigerate the leftover syrup.

10. Melt-in-Your-Mouth Cream Wafers

No matter the season, you'll find a reason
to make these delicate, delicious cookies.

Light, crispy, and flaky.

Gather

Cookies

  2 cups flour
  1 cup butter, softened
  1/3 cup whipping cream
  sugar (for dipping unbaked cookies)

Frosting

  1 cup powdered sugar
  3 T. softened butter
  1 to 1 1/2 T. milk or cream

  1/2 tsp. vanilla or other flavoring (such as almond or peppermint)

  food coloring for tinting (colors of your choice)

Make

Cookies

1. Combine the flour, butter, and whipping cream. Mix thoroughly.

2. Cover and chill dough for 1 hour or until easy to handle.

3. When ready to bake, preheat the oven to 375°.

4. On a floured surface, roll out about 1/3 of the dough at a time 1/8 inch thick. Cut into 1 1/2-inch circles or desired shapes with small cookie cutters.

5. Generously sprinkle granulated sugar on a large sheet of wax paper. Using a metal spatula, transfer the cookies one at a time to the wax paper. Turn each cookie to coat both sides.

6. Tip: to make coating the cookies with sugar easier, hold each end of the wax paper with sugar and move the paper back and forth to shake the sugar onto the cookies to coat them.

7. Place the cookies on an ungreased baking sheet. Or use parchment paper to make it easier to remove the cookies from the pan after baking.

8. Prick each cookie with a fork in four places.

9. Bake 7 to 9 minutes or until lightly browned on the bottom; the top should remain almost white.

10. Remove the pan with cookies and transfer the cookies to a cooling rack.

Frosting
1. Combine sugar, butter, and milk or cream. Beat until creamy and smooth.

2. Divide the frosting into several small containers. Add desired food coloring and flavoring to each.

3. When cookies are cool, sandwich bottoms of two cookies together by placing a dollop of frosting on one cookie and topping it with another cookie. This spreads the frosting between the cookies and keeps the tender cookies from breaking.

Shortcut: buy prepared vanilla frosting and add flavorings and food coloring of your choice.

Makes about 4 dozen cookies. Store in an airtight container. They freeze well for several weeks.

Variations

Valentine hearts: cut dough into small hearts. Sandwich two together with pink, peppermint-flavored frosting.

Christmas shapes: consider 3 colors for the frosting (red, green, and yellow) and 3 flavors for the frosting (vanilla, peppermint, and almond). You can also tint some of the dough if you wish, such as green for trees or holly and yellow for stars.

MELT-IN-YOUR-MOUTH CREAM WAFERS

11. Perfect Pancakes

Gather

1 cup flour
1 T. baking powder
1 T. brown sugar
1/4 tsp. salt
1 large egg, beaten
1 cup milk
2 T. oil
1 tsp. vanilla

Make

1. Mix dry ingredients in a large bowl.

2. Mix liquid ingredients in a medium-sized bowl.

3. Add liquid ingredients to dry ingredients and mix with wire whip until blended. Batter will be slightly lumpy.

4. Heat skillet and spray with cooking spray (or lightly grease with oil).

5. Pour 1/4 cup pancake batter onto the skillet for each 3- to 4-inch pancake.

6. Turn when pancakes bubble and bottoms are golden brown; cook the other side.

7. Serve with butter and maple syrup, honey, jam, peanut butter, or fruit.

Makes about 10 pancakes.

Variation: for buttermilk pancakes: replace the milk with buttermilk, reduce baking powder to 1 teaspoon, and add 1/2 teaspoon baking soda.

12. Royal Rings

Decorate cookie rings with sweet candy jewels—
to nibble, not wear.

Gather
1/2 cup soft butter (1 cube)
2/3 cup sugar
3 egg yolks
1 tsp. vanilla
1 1/2 cups flour
1/2 tsp. baking powder
1/4 tsp. salt
multicolored sprinkles
candied fruit or small candies that won't melt
   (such as Boston Baked Beans, Jujyfruits, or Dots)

Make
1. Preheat oven to 375°.

2. In a large bowl, cream together the butter and sugar.

3. Separate the egg yolks from the egg whites. Save whites for another use.

4. Add egg yolks and vanilla to creamed mixture, and beat until light and fluffy.

5. Combine flour, baking powder, and salt. Sift dry ingredients into the sugar mixture, and mix well.

6. Shape into 1-inch balls.

7. Push your finger through each ball to shape it into a ring. Make sure the opening is at least 1/2 inch wide so it doesn't close while baking.

8. Dip the top side of each ring into colored sprinkles. Place on lightly sprayed baking sheet.

9. Add a piece of candied cherry or small candy on each cookie for a jewel.

10. Bake 10 to 12 minutes or until golden brown.

11. Carefully remove cookies to a cooling rack.

Makes about 24 rings.

ROYAL RINGS

13. Sparkling Scepters

Crunchy and sweet.

Gather
thick pretzel rods
white chocolate chips or milk chocolate chips
large marshmallows or gumdrops
colored sugar crystals or sprinkles

Make
1. Melt chocolate chips (1/4 cup for every two scepters) in a small microwave-safe container.

2. Dip one end of the pretzel into the chocolate. With a table knife, spread chocolate over half of the pretzel.

3. Sprinkle with colored sugar crystals or sprinkles.

4. Push a marshmallow or gumdrop onto the chocolate-dipped end of the scepter.

5. Set it upright in a small container until the chocolate hardens.

WALKING HAND IN HAND AS CHRIST'S LOVE
transforms lives

MEETING THE
DEEPEST NEEDS

WE BELIEVE THE GOSPEL IS TRANSFORMATIVE
And you can change the world one child at a time.

Thousands of children in the world are born into a cycle of poverty that has been around for generations, leaving them without hope for a safe and secure future. For a little more than $1 a day you can provide the tools a child needs to break the cycle in the name of Jesus.

OUR CONTACT

 423-894-6060
 info@amginternational.org

@amgintl
6815 Shallowford Rd. Chattanooga, TN 37421

Made in the USA
Middletown, DE
17 September 2023